AFRICAN ETHNOGRAPHIC STUDIES
OF THE 20TH CENTURY

I0027978

Volume 22

THE OVIMBUNDU UNDER TWO
SOVEREIGNTIES

THE OVIMBUNDU UNDER TWO SOVEREIGNTIES

SOVEREIGNTIES

A Study of Social Control and Social Change
Among a People of Angola

ADRIAN C. EDWARDS

Routledge
Taylor & Francis Group

LONDON AND NEW YORK

First published in 1962 by Oxford University Press for the International African Institute.

This edition first published in 2018
by Routledge
2 Park Square, Milton Park, Abingdon, Oxon OX14 4RN

and by Routledge
711 Third Avenue, New York, NY 10017

Routledge is an imprint of the Taylor & Francis Group, an informa business

British Library Cataloguing in Publication Data
A catalogue record for this book is available from the British Library

ISBN: 978-0-8153-8713-8 (Set)
ISBN: 978-0-429-48813-9 (Set) (ebk)
ISBN: 978-1-138-58997-1 (Volume 22) (hbk)
ISBN: 978-1-138-59007-6 (Volume 22) (pbk)
ISBN: 978-0-429-49123-8 (Volume 22) (ebk)

THE OVIMBUNDU UNDER TWO SOVEREIGNTIES

A Study of Social Control and Social Change Among a People of Angola

ADRIAN C. EDWARDS

Routledge
Taylor & Francis Group

LONDON AND NEW YORK

First published in 1962 by Oxford University Press for the International African Institute.

This edition first published in 2018
by Routledge
2 Park Square, Milton Park, Abingdon, Oxon OX14 4RN

and by Routledge
711 Third Avenue, New York, NY 10017

Routledge is an imprint of the Taylor & Francis Group, an informa business

© 1962 International African Institute

British Library Cataloguing in Publication Data
A catalogue record for this book is available from the British Library

ISBN: 978-0-8153-8713-8 (Set)
ISBN: 978-0-429-48813-9 (Set) (ebk)
ISBN: 978-1-138-58997-1 (Volume 22) (hbk)
ISBN: 978-1-138-59007-6 (Volume 22) (pbk)
ISBN: 978-0-429-49123-8 (Volume 22) (ebk)

Publisher's Note
The publisher has gone to great lengths to ensure the quality of this reprint but points out that some imperfections in the original copies may be apparent.

Disclaimer
The publisher has made every effort to trace copyright holders and would welcome correspondence from those they have been unable to trace.

THE OVIMBUNDU
UNDER
TWO SOVEREIGNTIES

A STUDY OF SOCIAL CONTROL AND SOCIAL
CHANGE AMONG A PEOPLE OF ANGOLA

ADRIAN C. EDWARDS

Published for the
INTERNATIONAL AFRICAN INSTITUTE
by the
OXFORD UNIVERSITY PRESS
LONDON   IBADAN   ACCRA
1962

Oxford University Press, Amen House, London E.C.4

GLASGOW NEW YORK TORONTO MELBOURNE WELLINGTON
BOMBAY CALCUTTA MADRAS KARACHI LAHORE DACCA
CAPE TOWN SALISBURY NAIROBI IBADAN ACCRA
KUALA LUMPUR HONG KONG

PRINTED IN GREAT BRITAIN
COX AND WYMAN LTD, LONDON
FAKENHAM AND READING

To My Parents

CONTENTS

CONTENTS

CONTENTS

CONTENTS

LIST OF MAPS AND CHARTS

ACKNOWLEDGMENTS

The fieldwork on which this study is based was undertaken as a Research Fellow of the International African Institute between November 1955 and December 1956. I am grateful to the Executive Council of the Institute for awarding me the Fellowship and to Professor Daryll Forde, Director, and Mrs. B. E. Wyatt, then Secretary of the Institute, for much help in various ways.

Professor Meyer Fortes and Dr. Jack Goody were my supervisors during my period as a research student, their advice and criticism being the hammer under which my arguments have acquired some sort of shape. I must also acknowledge the great help and stimulus of Dr. Mary Douglas of University College, London, who contributed greatly to the revision of the manuscript for publication. I am also grateful for the assistance of Dr. V. W. Turner of Manchester, Mr. Charles White, who provided information on the Ovimbundu in Northern Rhodesia, Dr. Ernst Westphal, who introduced me to Umbundu, and Dr. and Mrs. Guy Atkins, who gave me much helpful advice and information.

In Lisbon the late Professor Mendes Correia, Professor Antonio de Almeida, and Dr. Roderigo de Sá Nogueira of the Instituto de Estudos Ultramarinos received me most courteously and were responsible for obtaining authorization for my work from the Overseas Ministry. Dr. and Mrs. Scott, of the Liga Evangelica, Lisbon, aided me with advice, introductions, and a much valued personal friendship.

I should also like to acknowledge the assistance of Senhor Norberto Lopes, at that time Director of Civil Services, the Archbishop of Luanda (the Very Reverend Moyses Alves de Pinho), Colonel Manuel Nascimento Vieira, then Governor of Huambo, Senhor Alberto de Oliveira Mendes, and the British and Portuguese staffs of Messrs. Robert Hudson and Messrs. Hull, Blyth and Co. (Casa Inglesa).

To Dr. Gladwyn Childs I owe both my introduction to the Umbundu people through his book, and his personal hospitality and interest. Other Protestant missionaries who helped

ACKNOWLEDGMENTS

me in various ways are Dr. Gilchrist, Mr. Henderson, Mr. Okuma, and Mr. Theodore Tucker. The late Padre Albino Alves, C.S.Sp., of Nova Lisboa, Padre C. Estermann, C.S.Sp., of Sá Da Bandeira, and Padre J. Feltin, C.S.Sp., of Bimbe, gave me advice, information, hospitality, friendship, and much kindness.

The people of Epalanga and its neighbourhood were most patient and polite to me. I must mention by name my servant, Pedro Epalanga Chimbalanya.

NOTE ON ORTHOGRAPHY

The orthography for Umbundu words used here is that adopted in the *Dicionário Etimológico Bundo-Portugués* of Padre Albino Alves. Generally speaking, I have used this for names of villages and of individuals (apart from Christian names). Towns, European settlements, and chiefdoms have been spelt according to the accepted Portuguese orthography. Dr. Childs has given all place names of Umbundu origin in his Umbundu orthography. Hence, my Cassongue is his Kasongi.

INTRODUCTION

The Ovimbundu[1] of central Angola appear under various names[2] in narratives by nineteenth and early twentieth century travellers in West Central Africa. In the present century three anthropological studies have been written about them by Childs,[3] Hambly,[4] and Hastings,[5] as well as two shorter studies by Bastos[6] and Santos Brandao,[7] and a large number of articles.[8] Despite the large amount of documentation available there existed a considerable number of gaps, especially as regards the political system and the kinship system.[9] In proposing to work among the Ovimbundu, I hoped to be able to fill in these gaps, and in particular to provide a study of what appeared to be a double-descent kinship system. I also hoped to study the reactions of an African society to Portuguese rule.

I arrived at Nova Lisboa in roughly the centre of Umbundu country in October 1955. Here, as in Lisbon, I was told that it would be very difficult to find an area where the traditional social life of the Ovimbundu as described in the literature

[1] A plural from the singular Otjimbundu. The adjective and the name of the language is Umbundu. The Ovimbundu people are entirely distinct from the Kimbundu people of northern Angola and the two languages are not mutually intelligible. However, the confusion between the two has gone so far that both Europeans and Africans speak of the Ovimbundu people and language as Kimbundu and of the true Kimbundu as Kamundongo.

[2] Mambari, Nano, Ovimbali, and so on.

[3] G. M. Childs, *Umbundu Kinship and Character*, Oxford, 1949.

[4] W. D. Hambly, *The Ovimbundu of Angola*, Field Museum of Natural History, Chicago, 1934.

[5] *Ovimbundu Customs and Practices* (unpublished thesis) 1933, D. A. Hastings.

[6] Traçaos Geraes sobre a Etnografia do Districto de Benguella in *Boletim de, Sociedade de Geografia de Lisboa*, 1908, pp. 5–15, 44–56, 81–99, 135–40, 169–76, 197–207.

[7] Articles in *Mensário Administrativo* (Luanda) March–April, July–August 1950, and Sept.–Oct., Nov.–Dec. 1952.

[8] See Bibliography.

[9] For an examination of the ethnographic material as it then was, see Merran McCulloch, *The Ovimbundu of Angola*, Ethnographic Survey of Africa. International African Institute, London, 1952.

could be observed. Eventually I decided to work in the Bimbe area, in the extreme north-western corner of Umbundu country. The census[10] indicated that Bimbe had a smaller white population than any comparable area of Umbundu country, and people who knew it considered that it was one of the areas most likely to retain a relatively conservative social life.

In Bimbe I settled in the village of Epalanga in the chiefdom of Gumba. The advantage of Gumba lay in the conservatism for which its people were noted in other chiefdoms; its disadvantage lay in its proximity to the northern boundary of Umbundu speech and culture, which led me to collect some items of ethnographic information not typical of Umbundu country.[11] On the whole, I am satisfied that the people of Gumba were in the past as in the present Ovimbundu in both speech and way of life.[12]

Many of my discoveries were at first negative ones. I could not find any evidence that there was a double system of kinship groups actually in existence; the villages were not composed of agnatic kin; the chief seemed lacking in power. Nor was it easy to obtain detailed information about the past even from old men. There is little interest nowadays in history, nor are the old social institutions regarded, even by those who once participated in them, as being necessarily better than those of the present day. The reason for this attitude seems to lie in Umbundu social psychology with its readiness to accept European authority and values. Interesting as the motivations behind this attitude are, this 'cultural amnesia' caused me much disappointment. I found it much easier to get texts on the caravan trade, and on ceremonial practices and proverbs, than on the political and kinship systems. The inadequacies of the information I received on the political system may be explained by the fact that Gumba is on the fringe of the area tributary to the old kingdom of

[10] Of 1950.

[11] The payment of fines by a man to his dead wife's kin had been formerly practised in Gumba, and still is further north. It does not seem to have been known in living memory elsewhere in Umbundu country.

[12] The northern limit of Umbundu speech is now somewhere to the north of the administrative post of Cela. As there has not been substantial migration from the south, it is reasonable to assume that it is many years since the Gumba–Cela boundary was also the language boundary.

Bailundo.[13] On the kinship system, however, I was even more disappointed. The information which I was given on the matrilineal groups formerly existing was much less than that provided by Hastings,[14] or by Childs,[15] and I have therefore not been able to obtain the detail for which I had hoped on the double-descent system.

Like all anthropologists I had a certain number of difficulties in making contact with the people, and to these were added the problems of finding underlying consistencies in a changing society. The Ovimbundu are not interested in genealogies and did not see why I was. My first attempts to take village censuses were regarded with great suspicion, and more than once people refused to give their names. Kinship terms and norms seemed to be and were very confused. Various matters, such as surviving pagan rituals, were concealed from me. My personal relations with the people were very happy, however, and almost everybody who came to know me was prepared to answer my questions at length.

My two great problems in the field were to obtain information on the old social structure (which I already knew in outline from the written material), and to see how the present-day society worked. The material in this thesis will be laid out in the following way. The first part will give an outline of Umbundu social structure as it was in the period 1874–1911,[16] that is, the era of the rubber trade. The second part will give a series of chapters on present day Umbundu society, which will provide the information necessary for an understanding of the mechanisms of social control. In the third part a detailed discussion of social control is made, beginning with an examination of a number of disputes. It is shown how the network of kinship and marriage ties in a neighbourhood provide local continuity and stability, while the wider units in which the Ovimbundu now participate are of European origin and control.

[13] Cassongue and Cela were tributary to Bailundo but were not incorporated into the actual kingdom (Childs, p. 168). Cassongue people say that they are not Va-Mbailundu.

[14] Hastings, Chapter VI.

[15] Hastings gives more information than Childs on the matrilineal kin group.

[16] The period of the rubber trade. Childs, pp. 202–15.

CHAPTER I

THE OLD SOCIETY

1. *History*

The Ovimbundu, who live on the Benguela Highland[1] of central Angola, have been in contact with Europeans since their emergence as a people in the sixteenth–seventeenth centuries. Dr. Childs has provided an excellent account of their history,[2] based on the collection of traditional narratives and a study of the published sources in English, German, and Portuguese.

The Ovimbundu arose from a fusion of two stocks, one that of the 'Jagas', a conquering race who invaded the Benguela Highland in the sixteenth–seventeenth centuries, and the indigenous occupants of the area who were culturally and linguistically related to the peoples who now live in south-west Angola.[3] The Jagas were described in some detail by the English sailor Andrew Battell[4] who was their prisoner for some time at the beginning of the seventeenth century. He tells us that they were warlike cannibals who recruited their numbers by taking adolescents from the peoples they conquered.[5] This society did not reproduce itself normally by descent since all children born were put to death.[6] He locates them geographically in the Amboim–Cela–Quibala area[7] to the north of the present Umbundu territory. Cavazzi writing in the later seventeenth

---

[1] In Portuguese, Planalto de Benguela.

[2] Childs, pp. 164–215.

[3] Ibid. p. 190.

[4] Ravenstein (Ed.). *The Strange Adventures of Andrew Battell*. Hakluyt Society, London 1901.

[5] Ravenstein, p. 33.

[6] Ibid. p. 32.

[7] Ibid. pp. 84, 85; Childs, p. 86.

century gives a broadly similar account,[8] among other information giving us the titles of some of the Umbundu ministers, thus Mani-Curio resembles Mwekalia, and Tendala Tjandala.[9] In the same period the Jagas appear in what is now southern Umbundu country.[10] According to Baumann[11] and Estermann[12] they raided and conquered some of the south-western people of the Nyaneka-Humbi group. At the end of the eighteenth century the Jagas and the Ovimbundu still formed distinctive groups, and in the nineteenth century the word Jaga was still used to refer to the Umbundu rulers.[13]

Ethnologists have shown much interest in the question of the origin and subsequent travels of the Jagas.[14] Battell tells us that in a Jaga camp of several thousand persons there would be only twelve or fourteen persons who were of original Jaga stock, the rest recruited *en marche*.[15] There is some evidence to show that the core of some at least of the Jaga hordes were Lunda from the kingdom of Mwata Yamvo. Thus the Imbangala people of Cassange[16] claim to have originated from the migrants from the Northern Lunda kingdom. Both Battell at the beginning of the seventeenth century and Pinheiro de Lacerda at the end of the eighteenth tell us that the Jaga called themselves Imbangala.[17] The Hungarian explorer L. Magyar collected in the

[8] J. B. Labat, *Relation historique de l'Etiopie occidentale*. Paris 1732. (Translated from the Italian original of Cavazzi.) For the Jagas see Vol. II, pp. 88–303. On infanticide see pp. 114–15, which states that all children born inside a camp and male children born outside a camp were put to death. Presumably female children born outside a camp were spared. Cadornega states that a woman was forbidden under pain of death to give birth in a camp. Is this simply a purification taboo which Battell mistook for a rule of general infanticide? Battell seems fairly reliable, and it is possible that there had been a change of custom between Battell's contacts in about 1600, when the Jagas were simply nomadic raiders, and Cadornega's contacts of about 1670–80, when they were ruling settled states. There is some evidence for such a change in Cavazzi-Labat, who dates it around 1648.

[9] Childs, p. 187.

[10] Ibid. p. 195.

[11] H. Baumann, *Paideuma*, April 1956, pp. 118–51.

[12] C. Estermann, *Etnografia de Sudoeste de Angola* Vol. II (Lisbon 1957), pp. 26–29.

[13] Childs, p. 188 and sources cited there.

[14] Ravenstein, Introduction; Childs, pp. 181–90.

[15] Ravenstein, p. 33.

[16] F. Travassos Valdez. *Six Years of a Traveller's Life in Western Africa*, London, 1861. Vol. II, Chapter V.

[17] Ravenstein, p. 84; P. M. de Lacerda in *Annaes Maritimos e Coloniaes* 5a serie, p. 486 ff.

Map showing:

- Luanda
- ANGOLA AND THE UMBUNDU KINGDOMS AT THE END OF THE NINETEENTH CENTURY
- R. Cuanza
- Porto Amboim
- GUMBA
- CELA
- NAMBA
- SANGA
- NDULU
- R. Cuvo (Keve)
- Novo Redondo
- R. CASSONGUE
- BAILUNDU
- GALANGA
- BIE
- Catumbela
- Benguela
- QUIACA
- HUAMBO
- GALANGUE
- NGANGELA
- CACONDA
- NYANEKA-HUMBI PEOPLES
- R. Cubango
- 1500 m. (4920 ft.) contour
- Administrative boundaries -----
- 0   Miles   100

Adapted from the map facing page 167 in Childs'
Umbundu Kinship and Character.

3

middle of the nineteenth century, in the eastern Umbundu kingdom of Bie, an historical legend which linked Bie origins to the kingdom of Mwata Yamvo.[18] Childs has suggested[19] that this legend was in fact not of Umbundu origin since later investigators from Serpa Pinto[20] (1878) to Childs himself (1938) have found that Bie traditions emphasized the local origins of the dynasty. This may of course be a case of the African tendency to manipulate historical narratives to accord with social relationships. It may be suggested that the Lunda traditions, which the core of the Jaga hordes carried with them, became diluted by the recruitment from the conquered peoples, and that the link between the Umbundu royal houses and the Northern Lunda were forgotten because the kings of the Ovimbundu felt no need, unlike the weak Luena and Ndembu chiefs,[21] to prop up their position by stressing their links with the mighty Mwata Yamvo.

By the end of the eighteenth century the Umbundu kingdoms that were to survive until the end of Umbundu independence were already well established.[22] In 1769 the first Portuguese fort in the Benguela Highland, that at Caconda, was established, and a few years later a king of Bie was to owe his throne to Portuguese intervention.[23] Trade in slaves had begun with the Jagas; but other items such as beeswax and ivory were bought by the bare-footed Kimbundu traders who came from the Portuguese settlements on the Cuanza (founded between 1582 and 1671); and by 1782 there existed small colonies of Portuguese traders in Bie and Caconda.[24]

Portuguese political influence was weak, and the kings con-

[18] L. Magyar, *Reisen in Sud-Afrika*, Pest and Leipzig, 1859, pp. 266–269.
[19] Childs, p. 173.
[20] A. Serpa Pinto, *How I Crossed Africa*, London, 1881. Vol. I, pp. 156–60.
[21] For Luena and Ndembu chiefs, see C. M. N. White, 'Clan, chieftainship, and slavery in Luvale political organization' (*Africa*, January 1957), and V. W. Turner, *Schism and Continuity in an African Society*, Manchester, 1957. For African attitudes to the recording of the past see J. A. Barnes, 'History in a Changing Society'. *Rhodes-Livingstone Journal* 1951, No. 11, Ian Cunnison, *History on the Luapula*, Rhodes-Livingstone Papers, No. 21, and L. Bohannan, 'A Genealogical Charter', *Africa*, October 1952. Mr. White informs me that the Luena regard the Bie kingdom as being of Northern Lunda origin.
[22] Childs, pp. 167–8.
[23] Ibid., pp. 174, 195.
[24] Ibid., p. 198.

tinued to engage in warfare. However, trade became increasingly important as the Ovimbundu realized the advantage of their position in between the coastal towns of Benguela and Catumbela, and the tribes of the interior. By the middle of the nineteenth century Ovimbundu were travelling throughout the area bounded by the Congo River, the Great Lakes and the Kalahari, and even transcontinental journeys were made. The Ovimbundu carried with them cloths, guns, and rum which they exchanged for ivory, slaves, and wax, to which must be added corn and palm-oil, these latter, however, obtained not from the far interior but from inside or near Umbundu land. The safety of the Umbundu caravans was preserved by the negotiation of treaties with the local rulers, and by agreements (not always satisfactorily kept) between the different Umbundu kingdoms.[25]

From about 1874 rubber became important in Umbundu trade, and it is in the period from then until 1911,[26] when the caravan trade collapsed, that the Ovimbundu knew a prosperity which they have hardly recovered today.[27] It is in this period too that there occurred both the loss of Umbundu independence and the establishment of the missions. In 1890 Ndunduma, the king of Bie, was defeated and deposed, and in 1896 Numa, the king of Bailundo attacked, disastrously, the fort which his predecessors had allowed to be established near the capital. In 1902–3 a widespread revolt, known as the Bailundo war, broke out against the Portuguese, the traders being killed, and the forts besieged. The reasons for this revolt, whose leader Mutu-ya-Kevela was a minister of the Bailundo court, seem to have been injustices on the part of the white population, and possibly a fall in rubber prices. After 1903 the remaining parts of Umbundu country were brought under effective European rule,

[25] Magyar, pp. 292–9; Childs, pp. 203–5.

[26] Childs following A. Bastos, *Monografia de Catumbella* (*Bol. Soc. Geog. Lisboa*, 1910, pp. 74–81, 105–9, 141–5, 180–5, 225–8, 251–5, 279–85) divides the rubber trade into three periods: the rise of the trade 1874–86, the boom 1886–1900, and the decline 1900–11.

[27] I have heard it said by old men who had taken part in the caravan journeys, and by a local mulatto trader that the Ovimbundu of that period had more clothes than they have now. For Angolan economics after 1911 see Henrique Galvão and Carlos Selvagem, *Imperio Ultramarino Português*, Vol. III, pp. 124–39, Lisbon, 1952, and Clement Egerton, *Angola in Perspective*, London, 1957, pp. 106–13.

5

and the European population greatly increased.[28] In some areas at this time a confused situation arose, in which 'robber barons', white and black, tyrannized over chiefs and villagers and engaged in the still vigorous slave trade, which now had acquired a few disguises on the coast.[29]

In 1911 the rubber trade ended, and about the same time slavery and the slave trade were effectively suppressed.[30] From this time onwards, too, civil administration began to be effective and the Benguela Railway became the most important link between the coast and the interior.[31] The trade disappeared, powers of the chiefs declined. The missions, both Catholic and Protestant, which had relatively little influence during the rubber trade period, gained more and more converts.[32]

2. Ethnography

Between the Ovimbundu and the sea lie the Hanya, the Nganda, and the Tjisanji tribes of whom little is known except that the Hanya and Nganda seem to be culturally related to the Ovimbundu.[33] To the south are the Nyaneka-Humbi group, cattle-keeping peoples who are culturally and linguistically related to the Ovimbundu, but who did not participate in the trade.[34] To the east lie the Ngangela[35], the Luimbi, and the

[28] Childs, pp. 210–11.

[29] For an account of Umbundu country at this time see H. W. Nevison, *A Modern Slavery*, New York, 1906. In Gumba I was told that Mutu-ya-Kevela the leader of the 1902–3 revolt had raided villages for slaves but that Samakaka whom Childs (p. 22) describes as a robber baron was spoken of favourably.

[30] Slavery had been legally suppressed from 1878. The slaves were called by other names but no effective change was made till 1910. See A. Bastos, *Monografia de Catumbella* in *Bol. Soc. Geog. Lisboa*, 1910 (pp. 74–81, 105–9, 141–55, 180–5, 225–8, 251–5, 279–5).

[31] Childs, p. 228.

[32] Ibid., pp. 220–23. Personal information.

[33] Ibid., p. 8.

[34] On these peoples see Estermann, *Etnografia do Sudoeste de Angola*, Vol. II.

[35] A tribe using this word as the root of the tribal name is to be found to the south-east of Umbundu country in the area round Vila Artur de Paiva. Padre A. Van Horrik, formerly of the Missão Católica de Cubango, tells me that the map contained in M. McCulloch, *The Southern Lunda and Related Peoples*, (London, 1951) should show the Ngangela as occupying much of the area actually assigned to the Mbwela and the south-eastern Ovimbundu. Mbwela does not seem to be the name any tribe uses for itself (Private information, Estermann and Van Horrik).

Chokwe.[36] These people are culturally and linguistically different from the Ovimbundu, whom, however, they have influenced, especially in the fields of ritual; the initiation rituals
typical of these people have spread into southern and eastern
Umbundu territory.[37] The Ngangela call the Ovimbundu
'Ovimbali', a name used in Angola for Africans who live with
or imitate whites.[38] I have heard an Otjimbundu use it for the
Kimbundu of northern Angola. The south-western peoples call
the Ovimbundu 'Va-Nano—they of the north',[39] but also
regard the Ovimbundu as being 'civilized'. Very little is known
about the peoples to the north of the Ovimbundu, who are also
different in language and culture and who are said to have more
rituals than the Ovimbundu. These are known collectively by
the Ovimbundu as Olongoya, a term with a rather offensive
meaning. Historically they are important for the Ovimbundu
since it was here that Andrew Battell knew the Jaga hordes, and
Umbundu tradition links a number of the chiefly lines to these
northern peoples. The Umbundu language seems to be gaining
ground in this area.[40]

All the neighbouring peoples seem to be matrilineal, as
regards descent, inheritance, and succession, with the exception
of the Hanya and the Nganda, who have (Dr. Childs suggests)
a double-descent kinship system, as traditionally the Ovimbundu had. All seem, as far as is known, to have had chiefs,[41]
though there were no kingdoms to equal the power of Bie and
Bailundo in the nineteenth century. Culturally the Ovimbundu
seem to have been ready to take over traits from neighbouring
tribes, and the Portuguese, and this particularly in the sphere of
ritual.[42]

[36] For the Luimbi, see C. W. Scott. 'A Note on the Luimbi of Central Angola',
Africa, October 1955. For the Chokwe see M. McCulloch, op. cit.

[37] Childs, pp. 115–16.

[38] A trader said that Otjimbali means a domesticated black. Estermann is
preparing a study of a Mbali group of southern Angola descended from Kimbundu
slaves.

[39] The Nyaneka-Humbi tribes use it for the southern Ovimbundu, the southern
Ovimbundu use it for the northern Ovimbundu.

[40] Childs, pp. 186–7; Baumann, op. cit.

[41] Baumann, op. cit. For the installation of chiefs in the Amboim area, see
Antonio de Silva Maia, 'Ritos e Ceremonias para a Entronização' in *Mensário
Administrativo*, July–August 1953.

[42] Childs, p. 220.

The great distinguishing mark of the Ovimbundu was their participation in the caravan trade. Some of the neighbouring people also engaged in trading journeys (e.g. the Chokwe) but in central Angola the dominant traders were the Ovimbundu by reason of their control of the routes to Benguela and Catumbela, a control which as Livingstone's narrative shows they tried for a while to turn into a monopoly.[43] With this must be linked the greater readiness of the Ovimbundu to adopt European ways, marked by the general adoption of cloths for wear by at latest the mid-nineteenth century.[44]

3. Economics and Social Structure

This section will describe the economic life and social structure which marked the period of the rubber trade (1874–1911). A genuine currency existed in the form of cloth, and fortunes could be made in it. Serpa Pinto tells us of one Otjimbundu who made £3,500 by trading in the interior and that he had met many men who 'turned over capital of a thousand to twelve hundred pounds sterling',[45] presumably in trade goods since Portuguese currency did not circulate among the Ovimbundu. At the capitals of the kingdoms genuine towns grew up. Magyar in the middle of the nineteenth century estimated that 5,000 people lived at Bailundo[46] and the British explorer Cameron who had crossed Africa from Zanzibar says of Ekovongo, the capital of Bie, 'the town of Kagnombe, the largest I came across during my whole journey, being more than three miles in circumference. On arrival I was met by the Kagnombe's secretary, chamberlain, and captain of the guard who wore red waistcoats as a sign of their dignity. The secretary was more ornamental than useful, being unable to write, but a subordinate, a black man and native of Dondo, was better educated and conducted the trade of Kagnombe with the coast'.[47]

[43] Ibid., p. 205.
[44] Ibid., p. 206, referring to Magyar as evidence.
[45] Serpa Pinto, pp. 161–2.
[46] Magyar, p. 391.
[47] V. L. Cameron, *Across Africa*, London, 1877. Vol. II, pp. 206–7.

The trade was conducted in caravans composed of up to several thousand people,[48] under the leadership of *entrepeneurs* called *olofumbelo* (of which the singular is *ofumbelo*). Of such were the individuals whom Serpa Pinto describes as earning wealth equivalent to a thousand pounds or more. Their role was to get together the caravans, to negotiate with the local political authorities, and to provide ritual leadership. The exact relationship between the *ofumbelo* and the ordinary members of the caravan is difficult to see. European travellers found that porters were content with low wages since they had opportunities for private trade, but apparently the caravan organizers had better opportunities for getting rich than had ordinary Ovimbundu. My informants stated that a man organized a caravan to gain wealth. A man who was in a position of prosperity would be known as an *ohwase* (rich man), would stay at home and be expected to assist his relatives.[49]

Different ages and both sexes participated in the trade. Childs says that boys from the age of nine upwards travelled on the caravans, and this is confirmed by Serpa Pinto.[50] Tucker, and my informants however, give the age when caravan travel began as being fifteen or over.[51] Unmarried girls travelled too, but simply acted as helpers to some male relative. The caravan organizers (*olofumbelo*) were old men, I was told, and travelled in the rear while in front of the caravan marched a young man (called the *kesongo*) who carried a flag.[52]

Dr. Childs states that between 1874 and 1886 rubber was gathered from the forests of the interior and took eight months (four months each way presumably) for the Ovimbundu to obtain. From 1886, however, 'red rubber' was obtained from the sandy lands beyond the Cuanza, a journey which only took three months altogether. Hence, Childs states, the trading

---

[48] A Bastos, *Monografia de Catumbella*, in *Bol. Soc. Geog. Lisboa* 1910 (p. 151) states that caravans of several thousand were used in the 1870s but that by the time of writing (1908–9, nearly the end of the trade) people came in small parties. My informants who would remember this period spoke of the large size of the caravans.

[49] My informants.

[50] Serpa Pinto, p. 164.

[51] J. T. Tucker in *Africa* (Notes and News), April 1956.

[52] Informants.

journeys diminished in distance as they increased in profitability.[53]

My informants, however, gave a somewhat different picture. Long trading journeys were still being undertaken in the last decade of the trade (1901–11). Some men whom I met had travelled to the kingdom of the Mwata Yamvo and beyond to Luba country; one man had made a journey into what is now the Congo Republic which took a year to go and a year to return; another had visited Barotseland. It should be said that these seem to have been unusually long journeys; journeys totalling six to eight months were common.[54]

The significance of the trade in social life is reflected in the mystical explanations of success in business found in Umbundu religion. Prosperity might be explained either by the favour of spirits such as Kandundu and Otjipuku, who received at their shrines libations of wine, or by malevolent sorcery involving the sacrifice of relatives in exchange for wealth.[55] The existence of these two explanations probably reflects the existence of some rich men who satisfied the expectations of their relatives and others who did not.

Apart from the rubber trade, the older slave trade continued until its vigorous suppression in the period 1910–12, and indeed seems, as regards the Ovimbundu, to have become intensified in the period after 1890. The slaves went to S. Tome and Principe, or to coastal plantations. Up to that time the Ovimbundu had sold few of their own people, with the exception of criminals or people who had become generally unpopular with their kin. The collapse of the old political system played into the hands of adventurers who unscrupulously exploited the Umbundu custom of debt slavery or conducted raids for this purpose.[56]

It was then the 'trade' which was the common factor in the life of all Ovimbundu, and which was so to speak the factor,

[53] Childs, p. 208.

[54] Informants.

[55] Although some old men still have shrines to the luck-giving spirits it is not possible to see how their cult functioned in the social structure then existing. It is, however, notable that success could be interpreted mystically in two ways by benevolent spirits or by sorcery.

[56] Childs, p. 213. I was told that Gumba had been raided from Bailundo.

rather than any political alliance or opposition, which related the Ovimbundu as a whole to the Portuguese and the other tribes. Informants who remember 'the time of the rubber' talk about it with much more interest and much more detail than about any other aspect of the past, and it is far easier to make an ordered picture out of the narratives of the caravan journeys than to fill in the gaps in the descriptions of the political and kinship systems provided by Childs and Hastings.[57]

Politically the Ovimbundu were divided, as has been said, into several kingdoms. Bailundo, the largest of the kingdoms was divided, according to Childs into about 200 sub-chiefdoms. As it had about half a million inhabitants this would give an average population of about 2,500. While the kingdoms seem to have been more or less stable in number and boundaries from the end of the eighteenth century, the number of sub-chiefdoms seems to have increased. Thus an official Portuguese estimate made in 1799 gives Bailundo as having only 82 sub-chiefdoms, and Galangue, where Childs counted 112 sub-chiefdoms, as having 78. The sub-chiefdom paid tribute to the king, sent men for his armies, and recognized his court as the supreme arbitrator. Some sub-chiefdoms were held by ministers or relatives of the king.[58]

It is, however, not easy on the sparse detail available to decide how much autonomy the sub-chiefdoms really had. Gumba, the area where I worked, was a sub-chiefdom of the Bailundo kingdom, albeit on the north-western frontier, neighbouring Cassongue and Cela, where the people did not call themselves Va-Mbailundu, though their rulers acknowledged the suzerainty of the king of Bailundo. Old men told me of raids from Bailundo for slaves, but I cannot say if this was the result of the period of disorder mentioned, or whether sub-chiefdoms on the border of a kingdom gave only nominal submission and received only nominal protection. In the area where I worked,

[57] This is not intended as a personal reflection on Dr. Childs and the late Dr. Hastings, both of whom deserve the highest praise for their work and for their obvious devotion to the Ovimbundu. Hastings devoted far more space to the magico-religious field than to the kinship system. Likewise Childs's description of kinship is much shorter, much less detailed, and much less satisfactory than his account of childhood and adolescence, or the really outstanding historical chapter.

[58] Magyar, pp. 385–92; Childs, pp. 23–24.

at least, the effective unit of law and self-defence was formerly the sub-chiefdom.[59]

In both sub-chiefdom and kingdom the chief (a term used here for both king and sub-chief) passed through a cycle of rites to become truly chief and was surrounded, assisted, and checked by titled ministers.[60] The future chief was selected from persons of chiefly stock. My informants stated that a new chief might be related either patrilineally or matrilineally to former chiefs; all other sources state that the chiefdom can only be held by somebody *patrilineally* of chiefly blood, with the exception of Santos Brandão writing on the Huambo kingdom.[61] The selection was the responsibility of the Mwekalia, whose role was to represent the people *vis-à-vis* the king, an opposition which is expressed in the Umbundu saying 'the chief is a guest, the Mwekalia is a man of the country'. When asked to explain this saying, the Ovimbundu point out that many chiefs come from outside the chiefdom, and also that 'If the chief does something wrong, we can send him away'.[62]

In such a constitutional deposition of the chief which nineteenth century observers describe as taking place fairly frequently,[63] the main responsibility fell on the Mwekalia. The cycle of royal rites consisted of the ceremonial entry of the chief into his capital and his taking of a new name, the rebuilding of certain shrines, a large-scale hunt, the building of an archway intended as a magical defence to the capital, and finally an act

[59] Informants.

[60] For the king and his ministers see especially Hastings, pp. 29–71 (based on Bailundo), and for other details of the royal court see Serpa Pinto, p. 167 (based on Bie).

[61] For references to patrilineal succession see Serpa Pinto, p. 159, Capello and Ivens, *From Benguella to the Territory of Yacca* (London, 1882), p. 81, Hastings, p. 42, Childs, p. 22. Santos Brandão (*Mensário Administrativo*, July–August, 1950) gives a list of the kings of Huambo where there had been two successive royal lines, and this shows several cases of succession by sisters' sons. (The Umbundu text he gives makes this quite clear.)

[62] The underlying idea is not so much that the chiefly stock is of immigrant descent but rather that the people of one chiefdom call somebody from outside to rule over them, who can be sent away if he misbehaves. Of course people living within a chiefdom are not excluded, but this point about the chief being a stranger is very strongly emphasized.

[63] Childs, pp. 22–23 and references given there.

of ritual cannibalism (*oku lia ekongo*) after which he could not be deposed.[64]

Hastings in describing the principal ministers of the Bailundo court states that the Mwekalia and the Galamboli or Ngambole (whose function was to remember traditions) were representative of the indigenous pre-Jaga stock, the Kesongo who was the war leader was a slave from another tribe, and the Otjinduli was of immigrant stock, and points out that these represent the three sources from which the Ovimbundu sprang.[65]

At the sub-chiefdom level some of the titles found in the kingdoms would be found combined, and the chief's court, where cases were judged, was composed both of titled ministers living at the chief's village and of the village headmen (some of whom were also title-holders). The sub-chief represented his people to the outer world, led them in communal ritual and judged, with his councillors,[66] their disputes. Hastings describes a case thus: 'When all the members of the court are seated in a circle, with an empty space in the centre, the plaintiff's counsel then relates the case, after which the lawyer for the defendant does likewise for his side. The chief in turn makes general comments. Lusenje, the official, whose duty it is to keep order at court and to announce the speakers, then calls on the accuser to come forward and make his statement.'[67]

While the sub-chiefdom was the largest unit in which law and order reigned undisputed, there existed alliances and cross-cutting relationships providing a contact outside its area. There was the *tjisoko* alliance which existed between two sub-chiefdoms which were separated by a third. Gumba sub-chiefdom was thus allied to Ndjandju from which it was separated by Chicunda, and messengers from Gumba and Ndjandju travelled together to Bailundo once a year to carry tribute. Apparently a sub-chiefdom had only one *tjisoko* partner. The relationship was one of funeral friendship; *vakwatjisoko* (*tjisoko* partners) undertook the burial of those who died without kinsfolk and also ordinary

---

[64] This is based on information from Gumba. See also Magyar, pp. 270–77; Hastings, pp. 43–45; Childs p. 21.

[65] Hastings, p. 60.

[66] Informants.

[67] Hastings, pp. 142–43.

funerals (though these burials could be undertaken by the cross-cousins of the deceased). When *vakwatjisoko* came to their partner-chiefdom for a funeral they had the right to steal small live-stock, such as chickens, or pigeons, but not cattle, goats, or pigs. An *ukwatjisoko* could sleep with the wives of his *vakwatiji-soko* partners without being sued for damages.[68]

The ties of kinship and affinity crossed the boundaries of the sub-chiefdoms and even of the kingdoms.[69] The members of the three spirit-protected professions, blacksmithing, divining, and hunting recognized obligations of hospitality to co-professionals from other parts of the country.[70] Again the caravans were so large that they must have involved people from many sub-chiefdoms, which presupposes a wide range of contacts.

It may be said that the picture given here is contradictory and inadequate. How can the existence of large kingdoms be reconciled to the extreme insecurity described by old men? How do the wealthy caravan organizers fit into the political system? What sort of politics were there in the kingdoms? It is not easy to answer these questions owing to the lack of evidence, and, probably, because the kingdoms were already in decline during the latter part of the rubber trade period. Indeed, the impression that accounts of the Ovimbundu in the nineteenth century give is that of adventure, battle, commerce, migration —a vigorous rather than a stable society.[71]

The kinship system is perhaps the field of Umbundu society which has aroused most interest among anthropologists. Childs and Hastings have written much that is interesting on the old double-descent grouping but as, with the kinship system, the form has been described rather than the functioning and it is

[68] Informants. The account in Childs, pp. 114–15 differs considerably. For this institution elsewhere in Angola see Estermann, 'Clans et alliances de clans', *Anthropos*, 1952.

[69] Childs, p. 54.

[70] Informants.

[71] Magyar describes the king and his courtiers as being extremely despotic towards the villagers, and states that their despotism depended on their having a standing military force called 'Sons of the Elephant' (pp. 278–80). Later accounts do not mention this, and Childs notes (p. 209) that at the height of the rubber trade it was more difficult for the kings to recruit armies for their wars.

not now possible for field work to supply the gaps in the written material.[72]

The traditional kinship system had neither clans nor segmenting lineages. The patrilineal group (*oluse*) was localized in a village, the group head being at the same time a village headman. Patrilineal ties do not seem to have been recognized between villages.[73] This social independence of the agnatically united village was reflected in the surrounding palisade, in the close clustering of the houses (nowadays much more spread out) and in the village institutions of the dancing-floor and the men's house (*ondjango*). It was here that all the men and boys, from seven or eight up, ate. Hastings writes, 'Each woman, after preparing the meal, takes or sends the portion which is for the male members of her family. This food is common property. As soon as enough has arrived some responsible member among the men will have it divided among the boys. For days a man may never taste of the food which is prepared by his wife.'[74] The men's house was also a club, and a court-room, where minor cases were decided. It was through this localized body of patrikin that an individual claimed land and residence rights and through it that he participated in the political system.[75]

The matrilineal group (the *oluina*) was composed of the descendants of a common great-great-grandmother.[76] According to Childs, it had a head who might also at times be a village headman,[77] and it was presumably the matrilineal group head who settled the disputes over property which Hambly says

[72] For an attempt at reconstructing Umbundu kinship on the basis of Childs's book see J. A. Barnes's review of *Umbundu Kinship and Character* in *Man*, 1950, pp. 126–128. It may be mentioned that the terms 'the side of the bow' and 'the side of the basket' are used simply to mean 'patrilateral kin' and 'matrilateral kin' (Dr. Childs, private information, and my own inquiries).

[73] A rather ambiguous phrase in Childs p. 43 ('The *oluse* consists of a large number of local village groups'), which might be interpreted as meaning that villages were patrilineally grouped into clans, seems really to mean simply that the village is the *oluse* unit.

[74] Hastings, p. 77.

[75] Ibid., p. 16. Childs, pp. 43–44.

[76] Hastings, p. 83, states that the matrilineal group consists of the descendants of a common great-great-great-grandmother (that is, five generations), and on p. 91 says that it consists of a group 'linked by a common great-great-grandmother'.

[77] Childs, p. 44.

C

could be resolved in the matrilineal group.[78] Hastings, who gives the most detailed account of the matrilineal groups, which he calls sibs, tells us, 'There can be no exaction of fines or taking of slaves between the members of a sib group—the group members are supposed to pay each other's debts, and one who has wealth and refuses so to communicate may be secretly poisoned by the others. It is within the group of matrilineal sibs that most compacts, whether social or economic, are formed and operate. The same is true even of malevolent plots and anti-social practices, such as killing by witchcraft.'[79]

Clearly, the matrilineal groups in which the rich had to pool their wealth with poorer kinsfolk and in which trading arrangements[80] were made indicate the adaptation of the kinship system to the needs of the trade. It may be suggested that one of the functions of the double descent system was to separate the fields of village and chiefdom relations, established through patrilineal ties, from the field of commerce, credit, and the inheritance of wealth gained by trade. Thus the conflicts in which a man would be involved in one set of relations would not involve his other set of ties, and this distribution of stresses must have limited the strains set up by disputes. The distinction between the local group and the commercial group would also prevent heavy losses from trade striking a whole village simultaneously.[81] The credit institutions demanded by a trading system in which debt was frequently incurred were fitted into the kinship system, and associated with a device for levelling those who had become prosperous in the trade.

Unhappily the disintegration of the traditional social structure, and the accompanying loss of knowledge of it, prevented me from adding to, or even corroborating entirely, the written material on the form of the matrilineal groups.[82] It is not at all evident how the groups maintained integration, or how new

[78] Hambly, p. 200.

[79] Ibid., p. 92.

[80] Dr. Childs suggested to me that the core of the caravans might be composed of kin. However, the caravans were so large that they clearly could not be organized on a kinship basis. See also Serpa Pinto, p. 165.

[81] This point was suggested to me by Dr. Mary Douglas.

[82] I did not obtain any information on the size of the matrilineal group, the existence of heads of the groups, and the degree to which it was a congregation.

groups emerged. The information on the cult of the matrilineal spirits which might have thrown some light on matrilineal conflicts and integration, is confused. Both Hastings and Mrs. Tucker state that the matrilineal spirits are always malevolent, but this is not confirmed by my informants,[83] and it may be that they were referring to the traditional belief that sorcery was only practised between members of a matrilineal group. Although, as has been stated, a man looked to his matrilineal kin for economic aid, he might travel with his father (who had first claim on his services), or with his mother's brother or some other kinsman; indeed while his father was still alive he might travel and trade on his own account.[84] The matrilineal group (in this area at least) was not a unit from which trading teams were formed, but rather a means for providing financial assistance when needed for those engaged in trading. It is of course possible that in some areas of Umbundu country the matrilineal kin groups were significant in the organization of trading caravans.

Another institution whose form can be described but whose function cannot be properly known is that of preferential marriage with certain categories of kin. Childs states that the categories were cross-cousins (both patrilateral and matrilateral), the sister's daughter, and the father's sister, and indicates that the cross-cousin marriages were not generally with first-cousins. My informants generally denied that it had been permitted to marry a father's sister, but confirmed his other statements. They added that an indemnification was paid by the bridegroom to the bride's family 'to cut the blood',[85] and that the kinship terms were replaced by affinal. This suggests that these marriages may have been intended to restore distant kinship ties by turning them into affinal ties and so renewing them for the next generation, but how this would operate cannot even be guessed.

[83] Hastings, p. 87; L. S. Tucker, 'The Divining Basket of the Ovimbundu', *Journal of the Royal Anthropological Institute*, 1940, pp. 171–201.

[84] Informants.

[85] This was paid down to 1949 or so in the area where I was. It was about 20 escudos, much less than bridewealth. It was formerly referred to by the Umbundu term for 'fine' (*ovimbu*), as was the payment made on the death of a non-kinswoman wife.

It was then the father who normally exercised authority over a boy, and on the father's death a child or youth would join the household of a father's brother. Yet the right of a sister's son to the inheritance of the movable property and to grants from his mother's brother was counterbalanced by the latter's right to sell his uterine nephew into slavery, a fate from which the father could save his son by ransoming him, in which case the mother's brother would no longer have this right.[86] In this society, the mother's brother—sister's son relationship was fundamentally an economic one, in which the sister's son received assistance in the trade and inherited his uncle's gains in this trade, but could himself be transformed into a source of capital.

I now summarize the evidence on Umbundu social control and its relation with the trading economy. It is clear that the Ovimbundu belonged to the number of those African societies with pyramidal[87] political systems and formal codes and courts of law, even though there exists uncertainty as to the relative power of the kingdoms and the sub-chiefdoms. Social control also operated through the kinship system, authority at the village level being in the hands of the head of the patrilineal group backed by the public opinion expressed in the men's house, and the dispersed matrilineal groups having sanctions in the right of sale of a sister's son and in the accusations of sorcery brought against those who failed to use wealth to aid their relatives. For the caravan trade to have attained the importance it did there must also have existed something of a *pax Umbunduca* stimulated by the existence of such ties as that between *tjisoko* partners and the 'international' hospitality shown to diviners, hunters, and smiths. Evidence of this *pax Umbunduca* is provided by the organization of caravans, and by the establishment of marriage ties between persons in different kingdoms, and between different royal houses.[88] However, warfare was not unknown between the different

---

[86] Childs, p. 44, and my informants.

[87] See Fortes and Evans-Pritchard, Introduction to *African Political Systems*.

[88] Hastings (p. 1) notes a marriage between the daughter of a king of Bie and Ekwikwi, king of Bailundo (1876–93). Childs (p. 171) notes that Kakulukusu, king of Ndulu, was a sister's son·of a king of Bailundo.

kingdoms of the Ovimbundu, though more frequently perhaps it was made against the non-Umbundu peoples.[89]

The question of the influence of the trade provides interesting opportunities for comparison. The Ovimbundu were the southernmost of the peoples who in the nineteenth century participated in the trade between the Europeans of the West African coast and the peoples of the interior.[90] In some ways the Ovimbundu seem to have been less influenced by it than were some of the peoples further north. The Ovimbundu did not develop genuine patterns of urban life as in Dahomey or Benin.[91]

Three explanations can be offered for the relative failure of associational groups and urban society to develop. Umbundu crafts were much inferior to those found along the coast of the Gulf of Guinea; there was no indigenous weaving industry, for instance, and the goods which the caravans carried to the interior were all of European or American origin, cloths, guns, and rum.[92] For these goods the Ovimbundu were dependent on the Portuguese settled at the coast or in the Highland and this meant that the Ovimbundu were far from economic autonomy. Again the trade had a relatively short time span—the real boom period lasted only from 1886 to 1900, and earlier on in the 1840's when the beeswax, ivory, and slave trade was flourishing, the Ovimbundu had plenty of time for warfare.

It would, however, be a grave mistake to think that trade had only a marginal influence on Umbundu society. It has been suggested that the form of the double-descent system owes its origin to the necessity to isolate economic relations from other social fields. In the sphere of ritual, there are some remarkable copies of European practices—for instance the holding of a feast in honour of the ancestors at Christmas-time.[93] Many ritual concepts are related to the explanation of business

[89] For information on Umbundu warfare see Magyar, pp. 277–80 and Serpa Pinto, pp. 177–9.

[90] See Balandier, *Sociologie Actuelle de l'Afrique Noire*, Paris, 1955, for a discussion of social change in other areas which had experienced a trade of a similar sort.

[91] For Dahomey see M. J. Herskovits, *Dahomey*, New York, 1938. For Benin see R. Bradbury, *The Benin Kingdom* (Ethnographic Survey of Africa), London, 1957.

[92] Childs, p. 206.

[93] Informants.

success. More generally, it may be suggested that the conditions of the trade in which wealth was dependent on contact with Europeans created not only the Umbundu esteem for 'shrewd behaviour' (*oku lunguka*) and their willingness for social change, but their marked docility and submissiveness towards Europeans.[94]

[94] See O. Mannoni, *Prospero and Caliban*, London, 1956, for an ingenious discussion of a similar set of attitudes.

CHAPTER II

THE CONTEMPORARY SOCIAL ENVIRONMENT

—————•ᴜᴠᴜᴠᴜᴠ(O)ᴜᴠᴜᴠᴜᴠ•—————

In modern Angola, an Overseas Province of Portugal,[1] the Ovimbundu form the most numerous of the African peoples, with their million and a half of population,[2] and have also the reputation of being industrious—especially the Ovimbundu of Bailundo.[3] Their homeland, the Benguela Highland, has also been of importance in the modern economic development of Angola.

On the narrow strip of coastal plain stand three cities[4]— Lobito, Catumbela, and Benguela. Both Benguela and Catumbela knew the rubber trade; Lobito was founded in the early part of this century as the coastal terminal of the Benguela Railway which runs through Umbundu country and beyond the Congo frontier and thence to Elisabethville. The Benguela Railway is the economic backbone of the Highland. On it are the cities of Nova Lisboa and Silva Porto and a string of smaller trading towns. Traders from the Bimbe area drove regularly down to Vila Nova, one such trading town on the line, a distance of a hundred and thirty miles or so to sell maize, and buy trade goods and African villagers knew that along the railway maize sold for better prices and clothes were much cheaper.

[1] This term was used for nearly a hundred years up to 1933 when the term Colony was adopted. In 1951 'colony' was dropped in favour of the old term.

[2] Estimate made in 1955 by Mr. Theodore Tucker then of the Missão Evangelica de Dondi.

[3] Galvão and Selvagem, op. cit., pp. 384–5.

[4] A city receives its title through official recognition. The 1950 census gives Nova Lisboa as having a higher 'civilized' population (7,382 of whom 4,756 were white) than any city except Luanda. The total population has been estimated at 60,000 (Egerton, p. 199). Estimates given me in 1955–6 suggested that Nova Lisboa has some 6,000 'civilized' persons and 20,000–30,000 natives. Lobito has fewer civilized persons but may have a larger native population of perhaps 50,000.

Most of the employees of the Benguela Railway are Ovimbundu and many of the old pupils of the Catholic seminaries and of the Protestant secondary school[5] have found employment on it as clerks and telegraphists. The railway has also become a means of Umbundu migration carrying Ovimbundu to work in the coastal cities and plantations, and on the other side carrying their speech with it to the interior.

Angola is economically a land of primary production, and its cities and towns are founded on trade. There is little industry, although Lobito is noted for its cement works and saw mill, and drinks, both alcoholic and soft, paper and pottery are all manufactured in Angola.[6] On the coastal plain there are sugar plantations and there are a number of other plantations especially on the western fringe of the Highland, but the main crop of the Highland is maize, grown by the Ovimbundu and sold by the traders to the official boards which have store-houses on the railway line. The traders have generally tended to scatter themselves over the countryside though now the Government is insisting on new traders settling in recognized hamlets. The towns are small and frankly rather dismal places, serving as the administrative and postal centres for the neighbourhood, with a parish church, a school, two or three hotels, perhaps a club, and occasional cinema shows and a number of stores with a rather wider range of goods than those in the bush. They are significant from the point of view of communications, linking the traders in the bush to the cities and the railway.

A network of roads covers the Benguela Highland with the result that all villages are at most only a few miles from a track which is usable by motor vehicles. A truck seen on one of these roads will most likely belong to a trader, though it might belong to an official on one of his rare local trips, to a missionary, or to a labour recruiter. There are now a number of bus services in the Highland. As these serve only a certain number of roads, villagers who want to make a journey of any distance must walk or thumb a lift from a trader (who will charge) or a missionary (who will not charge) or ride on one of the still infrequent bicycles, his own, or a borrowed one.

[5] At Dondi, with Dr. Childs as headmaster.
[6] Egerton, op. cit., pp. 151–2. Galvão and Selvagem, op. cit., pp. 334–8.

Men can go out to work in three ways. By going to look for work in a city or on a plantation, by being recruited in his village by a travelling labour recruiter (*angariador*), or by being recruited through the post for military service or for contract labour (a period of a year's non-voluntary work).

Men who are away at work may keep in touch with their kin by letters. These are sent to the nearest Catholic or Protestant mission station according to the religious sympathies of the sender and his kin and are sent from there to the villages.

Angola forms an Overseas Province of Portugal, and is therefore subject to the Overseas Ministry in Lisbon. The Overseas Provinces of Portugal are officially declared to be integral parts of Portugal, which is regarded as a nation existing in Europe, Africa, and Asia. The expression 'Here also is Portugal' is often heard in Angola.

The inhabitants of Angola are in legal status divided into 'civilized' persons, whether white, mulatto, or black, with Portuguese citizenship, and Portuguese 'natives' or 'uncivilized' persons,[7] this latter category including some 3,000 'uncivilized' mulattoes. The 1950 census gave Angola a total population of 4,145,266 of whom 135,355 were 'civilized'. This category was composed of 78,826 whites, 26,335 mulattoes, and 30,089 Africans, plus a balance of 105 presumably Goans.

The 'natives' are, unlike the 'civilized', subject to the Labour Code. There is no Native Legal Code, nor does Portuguese law apply to 'natives'. Administrative officers may apply Portuguese law, or native custom as known to them, or their own judgement.

The administration is headed by the Governor-General who resides at Luanda. The province of Angola is divided into districts each headed by a district governor. Both the governors-general and the district governors have usually distinguished themselves in the Services or in a legal career. Members of the administrative service are not usually promoted to these posts, although they may attain such positions as that of Secretary of Native Affairs.

The districts are in turn sub-divided into *concelhos* (a term

[7] By a law of 1961 Portuguese citizenship has been made universal.

23

which I leave in Portuguese since there is no convenient English equivalent) ruled by an *administrador*, and the *concelho* in turn divides into *postos* (posts) each in the charge of a *chefe de posto*. There is no specific limit either of population or of geographical extension for these units, and in actual fact very great disparities exist, despite the frequent revision of boundaries.[8]

Ovimdundu are found within four of the Catholic dioceses of Angola, though the diocese of Nova Lisboa is largely Umbundu as regards its African population. The Catholic missions to the Ovimbundu have been largely in the hands of the Congregação do Espirito Santo, and it is in this part of Angola that their work has been most intensive.[9] An effort has been made to build up a local clergy, and by 1956 there were some thirty-two priests of Umbundu origin. There is an official distinction between the Missions, which work among the 'native' population, and the Parishes, which are responsible for the 'civilised' population, that is all Portuguese citizens, whether white, of mixed race, or African; however, in practice natives come to parish churches, and 'civilized' persons come to Mission Churches.

Most of the Protestant missionary work[10] among the Ovimbundu has been achieved by a joint effort of the American Board of Commissioners for Foreign Missions (Congregationalists) and the United Church of Canada, though the Swiss Mission and the Plymouth Brethren should also be mentioned. The headquarters of the American–Canadian mission at Dondi includes a seminary for pastors, a boys' secondary school, a girls' boarding-school, the printing press, a hospital, and a leper settlement.

The American–Canadian mission has for various reasons been confined to the Ovimbundu though catechists from its stations have settled among neighbouring peoples; hence the Native Church it has founded is the only all-Umbundu social grouping that exists. Ovimbundu Protestants do, however,

[8] Galvão and Selvagem, pp. 235–40.

[9] For the origins of the Catholic missions among the Ovimbundu see Luiz Keiling *Quarenta Anos de Africa*, Braga 1934.

[10] For the history of the Protestant missions see J. R. Tucker, *Drums in the Darkness*, Toronto and New York 1927, and *Currie of Chissamba*, Toronto 1945. Childs, pp. 220–1.

meet other Angolan Protestants through such occasions as the Congress of Evangelical Youth, held at Malange in 1955.

While the Catholic missions are not tied to the Ovimbundu in the same way as the Protestants the number of their adherents falls sharply when the Umbundu boundary is reached. Responsiveness to missionary activity is a mark of the Ovimbundu today just as was participation in the caravan trade. Indeed, the main common possession of the Ovimbundu, the Umbundu language, is, as a literary vehicle and object of study, almost a missionary monopoly. Both missions produce a monthly magazine in Umbundu and Portuguese, and several books of a religious or educational nature have been published with Umbundu on one side and Portuguese on the other as legally required. The dictionaries and grammars are almost all of missionary authorship.

Acceptance of Christianity has also significance for Umbundu self-consciousness. The majority of Ovimbundu have come under missionary influence in varying degrees, and conversion to Christianity makes Ovimbundu feel closer to Europeans and superior to other African peoples. I have heard African priests claim that the Ovimbundu are the best people in Angola, largely on this ground, and at Lobito and Luanda tensions have been felt in the Protestant community between Ovimbundu and members of other tribes.[11]

The Ovimbundu live under economic, political, and religious systems introduced and controlled by Europeans. Yet trader, official, and missionary are all dependent on the Ovimbundu. The 'civilized' and the native live in symbiosis, and the two basic problems of this study are the nature of this symbiosis, and its relation to the social system of the native population themselves. To see this symbiosis in perspective it is necessary to describe what occupations and statuses Africans can hold.

The strict segregation of black and white found in South Africa is alien to Portuguese traditions. There is a lack of almost all forms of public segregation between white and non-white.[12]

---

[11] Personal information.

[12] In the racial discrimination that does exist the mulattoes generally count as whites. It is said to be difficult for a full African to obtain accommodation in a Luanda hotel, but the situation for mulattoes is quite different.

Added to this, the existence of the mulattoes[13] and *assimilados* (Africans possessing Portuguese citizenship) prevent social status from being identified with race. An analogy exists, however, with the social structures of the West Indies and Latin America with their 'colour-class'[14] systems in which there exists both a class system based on economic and cultural criteria, and a hierarchic arrangement of ethnic groups, the two systems coinciding broadly but by no means totally.

The occupational structures (that is, the division of the population into different occupations) found in different parts of Angola vary considerably, from Luanda, now nearly four centuries old, with its old mulatto families, and the body of cultured Africans who form the Liga Nacional Africana,[15] to some parts of southern Angola where something of a frontier atmosphere still survives among the traders, scattered among the very conservative pastoral tribes. In the Benguela Highland the native population provides the cultivators and unskilled labourers. At some points in Angola, notably at Cela, the government has attempted to establish colonies of Portuguese peasants who will not employ native labour. Apart from this all agricultural work in Angola is done by natives, either for themselves or for 'civilized' employers.

There are a considerable number of African craftsmen, some *assimilados*,[16] others not, in such lines as brick-laying, carpentry, smithing, tailoring, and so on. Some Africans with secondary schooling have become clerks, dispensers, interpreters, and telegraphists. Of late years, a few of the most advanced pupils of the Dondi school have chosen medicine as a career. Licences to conduct a trader's store are confined to the civilized population but even so very few *assimilados* seem to become traders.

[13] The word mulatto is considered offensive in Angola. The correct term is mestiço. The white population rose in the decade 1940–50 far more rapidly than the mulatto or 'civilized' African.

[14] See F. Henriques, *Family and Colour in Jamaica*, London 1953. S. Tax (ed.). *Heritage of Conquest*, Glencoe, Illinois 1952.

[15] The Liga Nacional Africana is an association of *assimilados*. There are other such groupings which act as benevolent societies and engage in cultural and social activities. For an interesting account of contemporary Luanda see Gilberto Freyre, *Aventura e Rotina*, Lisbon, 1953, pp. 324–41.

[16] The decision whether or not to recognize somebody as fulfilling the qualifications for the status of *assimilado* is very much dependent on the responsible officials.

While there are both African and white truck-drivers, this tends to be a speciality of the mulattoes. Business and professional men are usually white, though there are occasional Cape Verdians and Goan professional men, and in old-established cities like Luanda and Benguela there are mulattoes of high social status. There are no African *chefes de posto* in the Highland, though I have heard of an African holding an important position in the Treasury at Luanda.[17] The most significant section of those Ovimbundu who have received education are the Catholic priests, and the Protestant pastors because of their number, their social role, and their existence as groups.

There are, as I have said, some 32 African priests, and from 60 to 70 or so pastors. In the Catholic Church the most significant distinction is that between priest and layman, as can be seen by the courteous, even respectful manner Europeans adopt towards African priests; among the Protestants the significant distinction is rather that between the American and Canadian missionaries and the Ovimbundu members of the native church including the pastors.

While the white priests are members of a religious order and the African priests are not, both have similar duties and share a common life. The white and African priests eat together, pass their period of recreation together, and may alternate such duties as saying Mass, and hearing confessions. Both European and African clergy rely for their keep on the superior of the Mission. Three African priests have become superiors of missions.[18]

With the Protestants there is a division of functions, the missionaries providing supervisory and specialized services, such as agricultural advice, education, and medical work, and the Native Church being responsible for village work. Financially, this division involves missionary salaries being paid by the mission boards, and those of the pastors and the village school teachers by the Ovimbundu Protestants. Socially there is less contact between missionaries and pastors than between black and white priests. Many pastors live away from the missions at pastorate centres. The missionaries eat and pass their spare time with their families, and among themselves talk English,

[17] Private information.
[18] Personal observations.

switching to Umbundu or Portuguese for addressing an African, whereas Portuguese is the language used at the Catholic missions even between non-Portuguese.

The African Catholic priests then have approximate equality and identity of status with their white confreres within the hierarchic framework of the diocese of Nova Lisboa; the Ovimbundu pastors lack this equality and identity but instead possess greater independence and opportunities for leadership within the Umbundu Native Church, which functions as a partly autonomous body.[19] The difference in functions of the priests and pastors is related to the ultimate aims of missionary action; for the Catholic missions the establishment of a local clergy is part of the complete incorporation of Ovimbundu into the universal Church; for the Protestants the establishment of a local clergy is part of the building up of a totally independent local church.

I attempt later in this work to show what roles the missions play in social life among the Ovimbundu and in the relations between the 'civilized' and native population. Here it should be noted that it is the missions rather than commerce or the Government which have opened status-giving positions to the Ovimbundu. The clergy have higher statuses in the total Angolan society than do any other of the *assimilados*. They combine this high status *vis-à-vis* the Europeans with leadership in groupings which include the ordinary villagers, unlike the various welfare societies in which the *assimilados* associate.

So much then for the general pattern of cities, communications, and trains, of administration, missionaries, and traders. I now turn to the particular features of the neighbourhood where I lived. Bimbe is said to derive from the name of a princess (Mbimbi) who ruled as a vassal of the king of Bailundo.[20] Here at the beginning of this century Samakaka, a

[19] The missions provide supervision and specialist services including agricultural instruction, community development, education, and health. Village work and actual pastoral activity is the responsibility of the Native Church. For an account of such specialist services see M. F. Cushmann, *Missionary Doctor in Africa*, New York, 1944 and A. Strangeways in *African Women* (June 1956).

[20] Information obtained locally from 'civilized' people. Princesses were very rare among the Ovimbundu, though Childs notes that Sambos (Sambu) had a woman ruler early in its history (p. 178).

'robber-baron', established himself[21] and in 1904 there was a minor rising against the Portuguese[22] (not to be confused with the very extensive Bailundo war of 1902–3). In 1908 the government post was founded for Bimbe, and in 1928 the Catholic Mission was established at the point where the Bailundo Mission had the furthest flung catechetical school in that direction. In 1927 the first trader had settled at Chicunda.[23] The areas under the mission and the post do not coincide, but it may be said that Bimbe is the territory bounded on the west by the River Cuvo or Keve and on the east by the main road from Bailundo to Gabela. The southern boundary of the post ran roughly on a line between the post and the Ponte Salazar (which bridges the Cuvo (or Keve) and takes the road into Cassongue), and the northern boundary is formed by a parallel line drawn from the road some way to the south of Cela to the river. In 1956 the post of Bimbe was divided; much of the western part including the Mission was placed under a new post Luvemba.

Chicunda is twenty kilometres beyond the mission, and seven kilometres beyond Chicunda a turning from the main track brings one to the village of Epalanga. Keeping on the track, a further bifurcation, say two and a half kilometres on, gives a track to the left which leads to a small leper colony, and a track leading straight on and sharply upwards to the village of the chief of Gumba.

This village lies at the summit of a sharp ridge which rises up from the ordinary level and then drops abruptly to a neighbourhood inaccessible to motor transport, which forms the greater part of the Gumba chiefdom. The boundary on the other side is a river across which lies Cela.

Such is the lay-out of the area studied. It is up in the north-western corner of the Umbundu country, indeed down by the Mission, people said that the people of Gumba were not Ovimbundu really but 'Olongoya', as the peoples to the north are termed. Many of the people in Gumba had come from

[21] Childs, p. 22.

[22] Information obtained locally. I did not see official records.

[23] Information obtained locally.

Cela, and Cela influences are notable in several ways.[24] In Cassongue Umbundu has relatively recently ousted other speech.[25] Geographically Bimbe generally is rather lower than most of the Highland. Although the railway line and the growth of maize have been influential here, an alternative pull for labour migration is provided by the coffee plantation of Amboim and Seles, and by the coastal towns of Novo Redondo and Porto Amboim.[26] In the days of the caravan trade Novo Redondo was an important trading centre, more important perhaps than Benguela for the people of this area.

Work is sought by Ovimbundu in lands far from their home. There are Ovimbundu at Brazzaville; others have settled permanently in the Congo Republic, or work in Rhodesia; the Johannesburg mines have employed many, and some have gone as far as Natal.[27] In Epalanga, the village where I lived, there were two men who had been to Johannesburg—nor was this very exceptional and I am told that among the people south of the railway it is quite common.

The world picture of the Ovimbundu is vague, except as regards Angola and the neighbouring countries. The existence of Europe (Putu) composed of different nations Portuguese, French, and English is known, and I was several times asked if there were black people in England. Little or nothing is known of the other continents. The island of S. Tomé in the Atlantic is known, since up to recently Angolan labourers went there, and some convicts are still sent to it. Several people from the neighbourhood had lived in Luanda or worked on coffee plantations in northern Angola. The Belgian Congo was known as Bula Matadi, though people seem little aware of Rhodesia, and Mozambique (Portuguese East Africa) is confused with the southern Angolan port of Moçamedes. The railway lines and the cities along it are of course well known, and some of the people I knew had travelled to Kwanyama country in the far south of Angola to buy cattle. Johannesburg (Zhwaini) and its

[24] Notably in the arm ornaments and hair styles favoured by some women. Cela diviners are often consulted.

[25] Childs (p. 179) suggests that the change came about in the nineteenth century.

[26] For this area of Angola see Egerton, pp. 186–8. Galvão and Selvagem, pp. 378–80, 457–8.

[27] Personal information. Also Childs, p. 215.

mines are widely known to people. Although Ovimbundu Protestants are often referred to as 'America' a word used both as an adjective and a plural noun, they (that is, of course villagers, not educated men such as the pastors or teachers) have no clear idea of the existence of, still less any identification with, the United States.

Like the other parts of Umbundu country Bimbe has experienced much missionary activity. The Catholic Mission of Bimbe has had a great deal of influence, the catechists teaching catechism and leading daily prayers in the villages, which the priests visit once or twice a year, and at such feasts as Christmas and Easter great crowds attend the Church services.

The Protestants depend on the pastoral centres of Henge and Luvemba, which are regularly visited by a missionary from Bailundo. Both here and throughout the Highland Catholics are more numerous than Protestants, but in some sub-chiefdoms Protestants are in the majority, notably in Kapali and round Henge. I have already mentioned the differences between Catholic and Protestant missionary organization. At the local level a number of differences can be noticed, in such matters as the neater, more planned appearance of the Protestant villages which have far more rudimentary[28] (pre-primary) schools than the Catholics. These schools are entirely financed by the Protestant villagers; among the Catholics while there is a desire for more schooling there is a lack of the drive that the Protestants show. A *chefe de posto* said that Protestants spoke Portuguese better than Catholics; and the Protestants are more 'Europeanizing' in their outlook.

The *chefes de posto* visit each sub-chiefdom only once a year. As the relations between the *chefes* and the people are usually concerned with the gathering of fines and taxes, the recruitment of labour, and the arrest and punishment of offenders, it is not surprising that the people regard the *chefe* with fear and mistrust. Yet there is a genuine acceptance of Portuguese rule. Thus villagers sing the Portuguese National Anthem at parties, the Portuguese flag is a meaningful symbol, and there is a belief

[28] Rudimentary education is a course intended for natives at a pre-primary level. It includes teaching of Portuguese, and also some instruction in agriculture and hygiene.

that the Government is benevolent even if its agents are not, and men say that they like the Europeans. There are other opposed currents of feeling, though; thus a cook to a European family said to me, 'The Portuguese do not wish us to learn' and a villager declared, 'The Portuguese say to the English that the Ovimbundu have tails.'[29] The great mass of the Ovimbundu seemed to be without political consciousness, or desire for independence; there is little nostalgia for the days of the caravans, and it is widely felt that the present is better than the past, since there is more contact with Europeans.

Traders in the neighbourhood were relatively few, compared to other parts of Umbundu country. At Chicunda there were three trading stores and people who did not like them went across the river to Cassongue. Traders try to prevent natives who live in their neighbourhood from dealing at other stores where they can get better prices, but this is not always effective. Some Ovimbundu realize that variations of price levels are related to such factors as proximity to the railway line. The traders are criticized for paying their servants low wages as compared with those paid in the coastal cities. Although there is a great deal of mutual suspicion between the traders and the Ovimbundu which is expressed in the arguing and haggling that takes place in the stores, there is none of the fear so noticeable in the people's attitudes to the *chefes*. Many traders have a smattering of Umbundu, and have a certain affection for the local people. Economically, the role of the traders is to receive the maize and other products grown locally for transport to the railway line, and to distribute trade goods to the villages. Their presence is also important in preventing the rise of any other system of trading by markets or pedlars.

The principal goods sold are blankets, cloths, and clothing of all sorts, including fancy items such as sun-glasses. There are also a good many bottles of wine, and also oil-lamps and kerosene tins, and electric torches. For literates or would-be literates, there are pens, pencils, writing-papers and slates. Such goods as bicycles, gramophones, and sewing-machines are generally

[29] i.e. The Portuguese say the Ovimbundu are savages and keep them from contact with other Europeans. The Bailundo area had not (up to September 1961) been affected by the revolt. However, a marked change in this attitude of submissiveness seems to have taken place.

bought in the towns, and men returning from South Africa are said to bring all sorts of goods including typewriters. The traders do not lend money though they sometimes give credit. The living standards of the traders are often low, some being unable to buy a truck, and having therefore to come to terms with someone who has one. I have even heard of traders having to eat the staple Umbundu mush (*pirão* in Portuguese).

While the traders play an extremely important role in the local economy they do not establish any permanent face-to-face relationship with the natives outside their household and store, because they are not interested in them and have no reason to be. This does not apply in the same way to African *assimilados*, actual or self-styled, of whom there were a few in the neighbourhood, who lived more or less in Portuguese style. Of these one in particular, Justino, made a hobby of settling disputes, and will therefore re-appear later on. Their main source of revenue was coffee-growing, and they would occasionally have local labour working for them. As they tend to identify themselves with the 'civilized' population, their attitude to the natives is not unlike that of the traders, but culturally and linguistically they are linked to the Ovimbundu villagers, and if of local origin will have kinship links too.

This group is significant because it is in the total social structure of Angola a link between the 'civilized' and 'non-civilized' communities. Both the *assimilados* and those pseudo-*assimilados* who have persuaded the natives that they are *assimilados*, identify themselves with the whites but are also linked much more closely with the natives than any other group. As the division into 'civilized' and 'non-civilized' is legally sanctioned on the grounds of culture not race, a group which participates to some degree in the cultures of both sections must be of great significance in the study of the means by which the whole society is integrated. In the neighbourhood where I worked this group of Europeanized Africans were few in numbers,[30] both absolutely and in relation to other parts of Angola.

[30] I only know of one genuine *assimilado* in the neighbourhood though there were others who claimed to be such. Galvão and Selvagem (p. 408) remark of the Cazengo concelho of northern Angola, 'The great number of civilized negroes, some planters incorporated in the European economic system, hastened the disintegration and confusion of the tribal institutions.'

Their higher social status limits their contacts with the villagers without giving them positions of direct control. Hence they are not leaders in the native social system. They are significant for the culture of village Ovimbundu since they are one of the channels for the communication of European culture traits, and their very existence indicates the possibility of becoming 'equal with the white man''[31]

More significant than the *assimilados* as a means of linking the Ovimbundu with the whites, of the transmitting of cultural values, and of the creation of new statuses and groupings at village level, are the missions.

In the following chapters, the composition and degree of solidarity of the sub-chiefdom, and village, the network of kinship ties, the choice of marriage partners, and the means of social control will be discussed in their operation among the Ovimbundu who are inescapably tied to Portuguese rule, to world markets, and to the spiritual authority of the missions.

[31] I have the impression that in the cities there is some feeling that the status of *assimilado* does not give real equality but simply exemption from such burdens as road work.

CHAPTER III

CHIEFS AND HEADMEN IN GUMBA

━━━━━ᴧᴧᴜᴠᴜᴠⲞᴜᴠᴜᴧᴧ ━━━━━

1. *The History of Gumba*

The historical perspective of Ovimbundu is short. Few, even elders, know of any landmark earlier than the Mutu-ya-Kevela rising of 1902–3, nor even for those who had participated in it did the time of the rubber trade form a Golden Age by which the present is judged. The period about which most was remembered was the reign of Mbati.[1]

Mbati had ruled over both Gumba and Chicunda, a union which had existed only during his lifetime, and which would have given him on present-day population figures 7,500–9,000 subjects.[2] He had managed to keep in his own hands the relations between his people and the government post. Policemen arriving at his capital to recruit labourers were entertained while Mbati's ministers got together the men required. Although an upholder of the traditional rites associated with chieftancy he had been on good terms with the missionaries and allowed a Catholic catechist to settle in his village. One of his sons became a Protestant schoolteacher near the railway line, another entered the Catholic seminary but left and became a policeman in Cela. Many of the numerous progeny provided by his seventeen wives are still living in Gumba.

Mbati's downfall came through his practising the traditional annual ritual cannibalism (*oku lia ekongo*). About 1934–5 he was banished for this to another part of Umbundu country.

---

[1] L. Magyar marks a place called Gumba on his map (opposite to page 1) but puts it to the south of the capital of Bailundo. As he does not seem to have personal knowledge of this area, this does not rule out identification, especially as the Cuvo begins to the south of Bailundo.

[2] For the basis of this estimate see section 2 of this chapter.

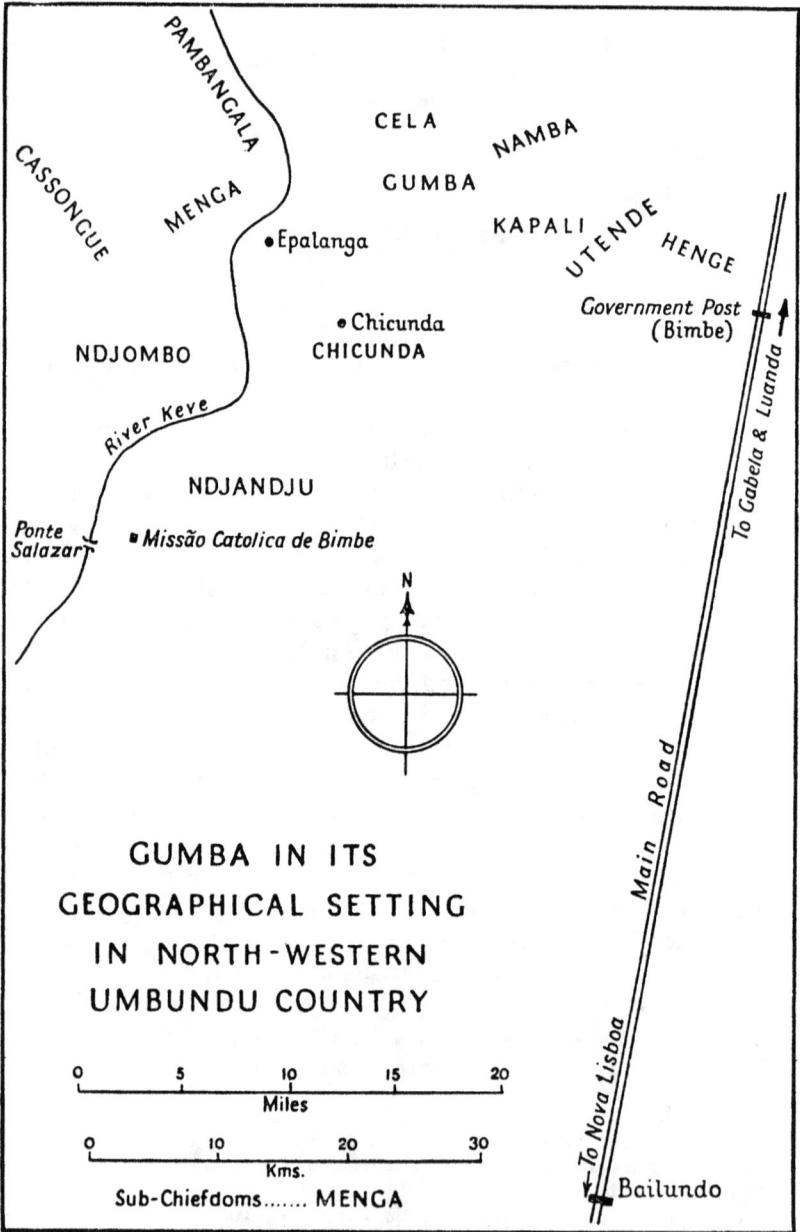

CASSONGUE

PAMBANGALA

MENGA

CELA

NAMBA

GUMBA

KAPALI

UTENDE HENGE

• Epalanga

NDJOMBO

• Chicunda
CHICUNDA

Government Post
(Bimbe)

River Keve

NDJANDJU

To Gabela & Luanda

Ponte
Salazar

■ Missão Catolica de Bimbe

N

GUMBA IN ITS
GEOGRAPHICAL SETTING
IN NORTH-WESTERN
UMBUNDU COUNTRY

Main Road

| 0 | 5 | 10 | 15 | 20 |
Miles

| 0 | 10 | 20 | 30 |
Kms.

Sub-Chiefdoms....... MENGA

To Nova Lisboa

Bailundo

36

Some ten years later he was allowed to return to Gumba but died on the way back.

His successor was Simbwyikoka, who was a mother's brother's son of Mbati, that is in Umbundu terminology a 'son'. Umbundu rules of succession allow anybody to succeed to a chiefdom who is paternally or maternally related to a previous chief, whether or not this relationship is genealogically traceable.[3]

Simbwyikoka was apparently nominated to act as regent during Mbati's absence, and as he did not complete the full cycle of chiefly rites he did not have quite the same prestige among the people as a chief in his own right who 'had finished', that is, had gone through all the rites. It was he who was the last ruler of Gumba to send the annual tribute in the form of a sack of fish to Bailundo, since it was a little after the time of his accession that Kandimba[4] (or Njahulu), the last of the Bailundo royal house to have any real authority over the kingdom, died.

Simbwyikoka had lived at the hamlet of Kamballa in Gumba. When he took up office he did not settle at Mbati's village of Katembo, but established, or rather re-established, as previous chief had ruled there, his capital[5] on the top of the narrow ridge which cuts off the greater part of Gumba from access by road. It was not possible for many people to settle on this site. Accordingly Simbwyikoka encouraged people to settle at the foot of the ridge, swelling the population of an already existing village. This was called Mwekalia from the headman, who held the office of Mwekalia[6] another ministerial title associated with the chiefly court.

In 1938 Simbwyikoka was deposed by the *chefe* for shielding his dependents from the operation of 'contract labour' (administrative recruitment of non-voluntary labour). About 1944

[3] My informants. This means that within (and outside) any sub-chiefdom there are a number of potential heirs who in no way receive any special status or form any kind of corporate group from this fact.

[4] Reigned at Bailundo 1911–35. Childs, p. 229

[5] In Umbundu Ombala, often transcribed in Portuguese as Embala.

[6] For the role of Mwekalia see Hastings, p. 59. His statement that the office is matrilineally inherited was not confirmed by my informants. It seems that it can be inherited either patrilineally or matrilineally. The man who was known as Mwekalia and had been headman of the village of that name did not function as such at the chief's court during my stay. A kinsman of his, Ngombe, acted as Mwekalia at the court of Lusase.

Simbwyikoka founded a new village known by his name. In 1951 one of his sons, Sassungu, founded a new village Sassungu whose population originated with a group of people from his father's village. Simbwyikoka maintained contact with Kamballa, where another son, Felisi, lived and herded Simbwyikoka's cattle.

The new chief was Kakope, a son of Tjiweka who had been chief of Gumba at the time of the Muta-ya-Kevela rising. He held office for only two years, being deposed by the *chefe* since ill-health made monthly visits to the post difficult for him. He was succeeded by Kafelo, who came to Gumba from Cassongue across the river. Kafelo was a cross-cousin of Mbati and paternal kinsman of Kakope. Having gone through the cycle of chiefly rites, and undertaken Mbati's funeral he was regarded as being fully chief, in a way that Simbwyikoka was not.

The Epalanga[7] of a chief is a minister chosen from among the chief's kin. Kafelo had nominated to this post Sapapula, a matrilateral 'brother' of his and an inhabitant of Menga. Sapapula moved into Gumba and founded the village of Epalanga in 1945–6, where he was joined by various kinsmen. I have heard the foundation of Epalanga ascribed to another man, Mwehombo, who will be mentioned again, and should therefore be introduced. Mwehombo had been minister at the court of Mbati, his mother's brother. After Mbati's death Mwehombo had stayed at Katembo till 1941, when he settled in Menga with his kinsman Sapapula. Mwehombo crossed over to Gumba in 1944.[8]

In 1954 Kafelo was deposed by the *chefe*, as Kafelo had been drunk in his presence. Kutenga Lusase, who had in 1945 founded the village of Kamupa, saw his chance and told the *chefe* that he had been chosen chief according to custom. The people of Gumba did not complain about this to the post, as they were afraid of the consequences. Kutenga Lusase claimed to be related to Mbati and Simbwyikoka and was a matrilateral 'grandson' of Tjiweka. He was not related to Kafelo whose link to Tjiweka was a patrilateral one.

Kutenga Lusase was in his turn deposed by the *chefe* in 1956

[7] Hastings, p. 53.

[8] Information from his 'brother', Luanga.

for lack of effectiveness following a series of quarrels. His successor was Tjilombo a government headman and the leading personality of the village of Tjisangu. Such, then, is the recent history of Gumba.

2. *Chiefs, Government Headmen, and Traditional Headmen*

I have outlined the succession of chiefs in Gumba, and the villages with which they were associated. I have noted that nowadays there are government headmen as well as the traditional headmen. I wish now to indicate what authority the chiefs and the two sorts of headmen have and how this is related to the villages.

The sub-chiefdom is a recognized administrative unit. The census, and the annual check on the census, are taken on a sub-chiefdom basis, as are the collection of taxes and the recruitment of workers for contract labour, road work, and jobs to be done at the post. The sub-chief and the government headmen have to visit the post once a month. The *chefe de posto* (head of post = District Officer) will normally only visit each sub-chiefdom once a year for the check on the census. He may send orders for the recruitment of labourers or the arrest of an offender by one of the policemen who live at the post. His principal contact with the people comes in the adjudicating of disputes which the people are quite ready to carry to the post—the Bimbe *chefe*, whose area included Gumba, told me that hearing cases was his main occupation. Very few *chefes* have anything more than a smattering of the Umbundu language, and they have only the vaguest knowledge of the culture and social usages—for instance they may be aware of the classificatory extension of kinship terms and the association of leopardskins with chieftancy. The *chefes* are moved about fairly frequently and their names and personalitie ;are not known to the people. As the people associate the post with demands for taxes, fines, and labour services, and are only likely to visit the post when recruited as non-voluntary labourers or to have their photographs taken for identity cards, it is not surprising that fear is the predominant emotion they feel towards the *chefe*.

The staff of the post consists of the interpreter, an African with primary and possibly some secondary education, the clerks who have primary schooling, and the policemen, who are often illiterate. The police are locally recruited and are provided with their keep, from the farm attached to the post, and with uniforms. They are usually—by no means always—illiterate. The interpreter, clerks, and police tend to identify themselves with the *chefe* as against the people; however, a policeman may be influenced in his relations with the villagers by gifts and friendship.

The size of population of sub-chiefdoms varies. The 1950 census gave the total 'non-civilized' population of the Bailundo *concelho* as being 246,045, and the number of sub-chiefdoms as 82,[9] that is, an average of 3,000 individuals per sub-chiefdom. The *chefe* of Bimbe told me in August 1956 that Gumba had 800 taxpayers, and Chicunda had 700. Putting the proportion of taxpayers as 1 to 6 (on the basis of Epalanga proportions) this gives 4,800 as the population figure for Gumba and 4,200 as the figure for Chicunda. Even if the proportion of 1 to 5 be taken as the proportion between taxpayers and total population this gives us 4,000 as the figure for Gumba and 3,500 as the figure for Chicunda. I do not know what the local density of population is; in the Bailundo *concelho* as a whole it is 16–17 individuals per square kilometre.[10]

The chief and government headmen are the main channel of conveying demands and orders from the post to the villagers. They receive in return the remission of their taxes. Their dependence on the post is not, however, sufficient to give them a position of marked superiority in their locality for the following reasons. They are unable to control all relations between the post and the people; anybody who has a dispute on hand may take it direct to the post. In village life their influence can always be counterbalanced by that of the catechists and 'elders of the school' whose contact with the missions is much closer than that of the chiefs and government headmen with the post. They also lack economic resources; the exemption from taxes (which the Catholic catechists share)

[9] See Gálvao and Selvagem, pp. 384–5. For Angolan population density see Egerton, pp. 36–37.

[10] My own estimate from figures given by Galvão and Selvagem.

does not give them any claim to financial assistance from the people, or control over natural resources, such as land rights. The only prerogative of this sort that the chief has is the right to the leg of an antelope killed in a hunt or a bull killed in a commemoration rite—and this is of symbolic rather than economic importance.

Nor, finally, does the post give the chiefs prestige and support.[11] Five successive chiefs of Gumba had been deposed by the post, and it is not uncommon for chiefs and government headmen to be beaten or otherwise punished (for instance by being made to work for a fortnight at the post) for their shortcomings. They have in fact just sufficient power to carry out the commands of the *chefe* and to do nothing more. They are not disliked by the local people for doing what the *chefe* tells them to do, but any attempt at dictatorial behaviour on their part will stir up opposition which may lead to their downfall.

The relations between white *chefe* and black chief vary according to individuals and neighbourhoods. Sometimes the *chefe* will allow the chief to be chosen according to tradition; at other times he will impose a candidate of his own. A *chefe* may hear any cases that are brought to the post, or he may delegate the power of hearing minor cases to the chiefs. Some *chefes* will regard the chiefs with hostility as being enemies of their own people; others will abstain under any circumstances from beating a chief, as they feel their power should be supported. Here I describe the situation as it was in Gumba and in Bimbe generally.

A visit to a chief's village in Gumba or elsewhere will give an opportunity of meeting those residents who hold the ministerial titles, of gazing under overshadowing trees at the enclosure in which are kept the skulls of former chiefs, and perhaps of seeing the chief and some of his cronies dance to a drum in commemoration of one of his predecessors. Ministers, skulls, dances, and drum are symbols of chiefly nostalgia rather than of political power. The ceremonies have little interest for the people in general, and many of them have been abandoned by the chief. Lusase's first wife had not, as custom demanded,

[11] For criticism of this policy by two Portuguese with administrative experience see Galvão and Selvagem, p. 213.

become *inakulu* (queen) because she feared the unpleasant haunting by the spirits of former queens which is traditionally experienced by the holder of this office.[12] On one occasion Lusase himself offered to let me into the *akokoto* (the enclosure where the skulls of dead chiefs were kept) for the payment of five or ten escudos (1s. 3d. or 2s. 6d.) although the entry of anybody except the chief and possibly certain of his courtiers appears traditionally to have been forbidden under the penalty of death sent by the spirits. Even the surviving rites are confined to the chief's village; the first-fruits ceremony in which the whole chiefdom was involved disappeared a number of years ago. The association general in Umbundu country between the chiefs and paganism does not provide an added ritual sanction to the chief's power, but rather links him with what is felt to be a dying past, essentially unimportant, at the present day.

The chief may also have some of his time occupied with hearing cases. A good many minor disputes are solved by local adjudication, but there seems to be no specific division between cases that ought to come to the chief and those which can be arbitrated by somebody else. Elders from outside a chiefdom may be invited to adjudicate on a particular case. The old formality of legal procedure has largely disappeared, probably because all disputes at a local level can be carried to the post— hence any ruling by chief or elders is essentially dependent on its acceptance by the disputants.

Accusations of sorcery are rather different from other cases since the post does not believe them although such an accusation is not in itself punishable. Sometimes suspected sorcerers are accused at the post of 'poisoning'.[13] Lusase told me that convicted sorcerers were fined a chicken, a goat and a pig. Gregorio, the chief of Menga, at first said, when I asked about this, that it was not possible to know who was a sorcerer. When, rather to his surprise, I mentioned the traditional basket test, he agreed and explained that people convicted by this test were sent as labourers to the post to satisfy whatever demand was being made for workers.

[12] Informants. See also Hastings, p. 49.
[13] Childs, p. 58.

The tasks of recruiting contract labourers and road-workers and of getting fines and taxes paid, and such other duties as the arranging of compulsory purchase of tickets for the travelling cinema (showing patriotic films) are carried out through a long process of argument, attempted evasion, and pressure, between the chief, the government headmen, and the locally influential people, traditional headmen, catechists, and anyone else who can get himself listened to. Persons actually picked for contract labour or road work may make quite a fuss about it, but as such numbers are recruited it is ultimately accepted resignedly. It is not really practicable for a chief to discriminate in favour of his kinsman owing to the heavy demands for labour and the likelihood of such discrimination being reported at the post, as happened to Simbwyikoka. Demands for labour may fall heavily on some households. Thus one Epalanga household consisted of a man, his daughter by an earlier marriage, his wife and her baby daughter. The man had been taken for contract labour, his wife had been called to road work, and the adolescent daughter was carrying sisal[14] to the post. A kinsman of the household head attempted to arrange for some watch to be kept over the gardens lest animals should get in.

There were four government headmen in Gumba during my stay. Theoretically they are village headmen. The villages in which official records group Ovimbundu do not conform to the actual villages in which Ovimbundu live. Anybody moving from one village to another has to pay a fee; as the Ovimbundu move about quite frequently and no attempt is made to enforce this rule locally, the result is this discrepancy between paper and real villages.

The government headman's duties are those already described for the chief. As with the chief, there is only sufficient backing from the post for him to carry out the orders he receives; he does not receive power to enable him to exercise political leadership and judicial authority at the local level, nor is he a representative of the post in the villages. His interests and values are linked to those of his neighbours rather than to the post. It is through the chief and the government headmen

[14] Some villages are obliged to grow sisal and take it to the post without payment.

43

that the administration gets labour and money from the villagers, and largely though not exclusively through them that the villagers keep in touch with the post which politically integrates them into Angola and legally provides sanctions which they do not possess. The government headmen do not supervise on behalf of the post the daily life of their fellow-villagers. The government laws—such as the prohibition of beer- and rum-brewing and grass-burning (for hunts)—which if enforced would bring about a certain number of changes in Umbundu social life, are not enforced for many reasons—the administration makes no real attempt to suppress these uses as opposed to levying annual fines[15] per head, the government headmen go in for these customs themselves, and they lack the power to achieve this enforcement. Were the government to introduce policies involving some reorganization of the social life they would need a stronger form of local authority. Under the present circumstances, however, the powers and status of the chief and government headmen are quite consistent with the demands made on them by the post.

There were four government headmen in Gumba in 1955-6, Guilherme, Lupassa, Tjilombo (who became chief after the deposition of Lusase), and Walivanga. Guilherme was in 1955 living in Epalanga. Some people thought he should live in Kamupa which had been founded by his mother's brother Lusase—however, when he left Epalanga in 1956 he settled near the Protestant village of Kalungwengwe. His change of residence had been the result of violent quarrels with Paulo and other Epalanga people. Lupassa lived in Katembo, and was a sister's son of Kaluywa, who was the traditional headman. I do not think Lupassa was the dominating personality in Katembo. Tjilombo was on the other hand the leading personality in Tjisangu, many of its people being related to him. Walivanga was similarly linked by kin or affinal ties to the majority of the people of Belem.

The foregoing paragraph raises the question of the relationship of the government headman to the traditional headmen. A man who is both a government headman and a traditional headman is in a fairly strong position in his village; when the

[15] Each fine is about 10–20 escudos (2/6d.–5/-).

government headman is not the same person as the traditional headman he may become involved in quarrels unless he is careful to accept the position of the traditional headman; and both government headman and traditional headman may find it wise to be on good terms with the catechist and the elder of the school.

It is fairly simple to define the obligations of the government headman. Discussing the position of the traditional headman vague words such as 'influence' and 'prestige' must be used to describe a vague position. Indeed a purely synchronic picture would be inadequate, since the present position of the traditional headmen and the contemporary village organization must be understood against a historical background.

3. Headmen and Their Villages

In the time of the rubber trade the village headman was both the leader of a body of agnatic kinsmen and the representative of his village in the wider political system, the village headmen sitting with the chief to judge cases. Both Childs and Hambly emphasize the importance of the judicial role of the village headmen. Childs states that the village headman was also a ritual leader, being responsible for 'regular village worship including agricultural festivals'.[16] I have found no evidence of such ceremonies on a village basis. The only ritual which, according to my older informants, the village headman should perform for his people is communing with his ancestor spirits in the spirit hut during a village hunt, and this information was not confirmed by all my older informants. It may be added that I found no evidence of any installation rite for a new headman.

It may be assumed that a good deal of the old village structure survived till the middle or end of the 1930's. Dr. Childs in his description of the village of Ngendo (Cassongue) as it was in 1935–6 indicated that agnatic kinship was the main principle of village recruitment, and that this was typical of other Umbundu villages.[17] In Gumba it was still possible at this time

[16] Childs, p. 46.
[17] Ibid., pp. 25–37.

for individuals to build up large villages—thus Simbwyikoka encouraged people to settle at Mwekalia to make it a large village. It may also be suggested that the power of the village headmen was to some extent linked with the power of the chief, since the headmen were associated politically with the chief, and would from this, tend to gain authority in their dealings with their fellow villagers. The village headmen also lacked any real competition from other types of leadership. Mbati had kept relations with the post in his own hands, and there were therefore no government headmen. The first catechist had arrived in Mbati's village in 1928, but cannot have met with much lasting success as there are few baptized Christians over thirty-five in Gumba.

Other factors at the time strengthening the position of the village headmen were the low rate of labour migration[18] and the fact that practically every man over forty at the time of Simbwyikoka's accession had participated in the rubber trade. This meant that many of the best known caravan leaders were still in full vigour, and enjoyed a prestige based on the first-hand knowledge of the middle-aged and older men.

Between this period of the middle thirties and the beginning of my own fieldwork twenty years had passed and many changes had taken place. The status of the chief had sharply declined and he was now assisted by the four government headmen. Every village except the chief's village had a Catholic or Protestant catechist, and there had been a marked trend towards learning catechism in preparation for baptism, which had begun about 1946. Hence the catechetical school was usually attended by the majority of under twenty-five's in the village.

Agnatic kinship had ceased to be the principle of village membership. Nor can it be said that headmen build up villages by getting people to settle at a particular spot. It is not always easy even to find the headman, village population is not very stable, and a man can settle with any category of kin.

To discover the traditional headman required careful phrasing of questions. When I visited a village and asked for the osekulu yimbo (the traditional phrase for the village headman) I

[18] Ibid., p. 214.

might be told that he lived elsewhere. This would turn out to be a reference to the government headman. A request for the *osekulu* (literally elder father, hence elder or headman) might also bring me in contact with the 'elder of the school', the representative of the local Christians. I therefore began to ask for 'the old one' (*ukulu*), or to inquire 'Who built first?' or 'Who settles disputes?', when I wanted to find out who was the traditional headman.

Even these questions did not necessarily get a clear answer. Thus the village of Kamupa had been founded by Lusase, its government headman was Guilherme, and, as neither of these was living near, minor disputes were referred to two old men who lived in the village. Apart from the government headmen, there are also traditional headmen recognized by the post, who did not have the privileges and the duties of the former. It may happen in a particular village that the man recognized as traditional headman by the post is not the same person as the real traditional headman recognized by the village. This was the case in Epalanga, where Sapapula was unquestionably the headman recognized by the villagers but the duties of dealing with policemen fell to Luanga. In the local discussions as to the recruitment of road-workers, and so on, Sapapula had much more influence than Luanga.

The position of the traditional headman nowadays lacks clearly defined powers, or symbolic value. A village is frequently known by its founder's name. The headman is the only person who can speak of 'my village' as opposed to 'our village'.[19] The firing of the long grass in the dry season which marks the beginning of the great communal hunts is theoretically begun by the village headman, though this is not always adhered to in practice. The headman does not take any active part in leading the hunt, nor are the people who go on a communal hunt necessarily confined to the inhabitants of one village. He has 'to show land' to new-comers to the village. This reflects a moral responsibility to his people rather than control of land tenure, since there is always spare land away from the villages which anybody can cultivate. He also has the responsibility of hearing minor disputes. He receives from the

[19] Ibid., pp. 36-37.

E

47

villagers a certain, not very marked, respect, which may be increased by such factors as kinship ties between him and them, and his personal qualities.

Nor is the village itself clearly defined as a social unit. It does not possess any corporate rights over fishing and hunting sites, or control access to firewood gathering. A man may hold land in two villages. It is rarely that a village acts or is treated as a unit. The two main occasions on which the village is thus 'represented' are at marriages and in the context of the catechetical school. The party which goes from the bridegroom's village to the bride's represents her village, to the other village; at the wedding feast food is given out on large basket plates, one for each village represented among the guests.

The role of the catechetical school as representative of the village as a whole will be discussed in another chapter; here it should be noted that the ceremonial reception of visiting missionaries by the 'school people' of the village has been evidently copied to some extent from the welcome given to the bridegroom's party, and this has in turn copied certain features from the welcoming of missionaries—notably the use of speeches in Portuguese.

The hamlets[20] and isolated households do not indicate a modernizing 'individualistic' trend away from village life, since 'conservative' and 'progressive' people are to be found in both units of residence. The Ovimbundu, whether educated or illiterate, when talking about themselves (particularly in comparison with the Kimbundu of Northern Angola) emphasize that they are a village-dwelling people, and for them the real values of village life seem to be the sociability and mutual help that a man living among his kin can enjoy. By settling in a village one indicates where the pull of kinship ties is strongest rather than any particular allegiance to the village headman.

[20] I use this term for a settlement with less than four households.

CHAPTER IV

THE INTERNAL STRUCTURE
OF VILLAGES

———◦≈≈≈≈≈≈◦⦿◦≈≈≈≈≈≈◦———

1. *The Village Epalanga*

In this chapter the internal social relations of the village and the relevance to them of the headman will be examined.

Epalanga, which has been mentioned as associated with Sapapula, the Epalanga of the former chief Kafelo, was a village of 148 inhabitants living in 36 households. Its houses stretched from near the River Keve (or Cuvo) to near the track leading to Chicunda, a distance of between half and two-thirds of a mile. Its layout is of the untidy scattered sort typical of most Umbundu villages, indeed its size leads it to be more scattered and spread out than is usual. Houses are surrounded by their own gardens in which maize and other crops are grown, and there are a number of stretches of bush in between homesteads.

Four main sources of origin (as regards kinship ties not as regards localities) for Epalanga may be noted. The largest 'kinship core'[1] was composed of Sapapula and his kin numbering 16 households. The second largest was that of the kin of Mwehombo (who was a matrilateral 'brother'[2] of Sapapula) and Mbati the former chief of Gumba and mother's brother

---

[1] This term seems more satisfactory than 'cluster' which has a local meaning, or 'group' which suggests an unilineal descent group. It is not intended to give a term indicating a unit with defined boundaries. Childs notes that *imbo* (village) can also be used as a word for a cluster of houses within a village. He also gives the word *ocitawila* for a ward within a village. This word was not known locally.

[2] I have employed inverted commas to indicate classificatory use of terms which for European refer to the members of the elementary family, e.g. matrilateral 'brother'. I have not done so where the classificatory use relates to a term not associated with the elementary family, e.g. mother's brother. In ordinary social life there is no great distinction between a 'true' and a 'classificatory' mother's brother.

of both Mwehombo and Sapapula. The third grouping was that of Ndjoleya (who was not directly related to Mwhombo or Sapapula) and his kin. Finally there were some people who were linked to Lusase (chief of Gumba 1954–6) who was not and had apparently never been an inhabitant of Epalanga, plus a few individuals who cannot be fitted on to any kinship core.

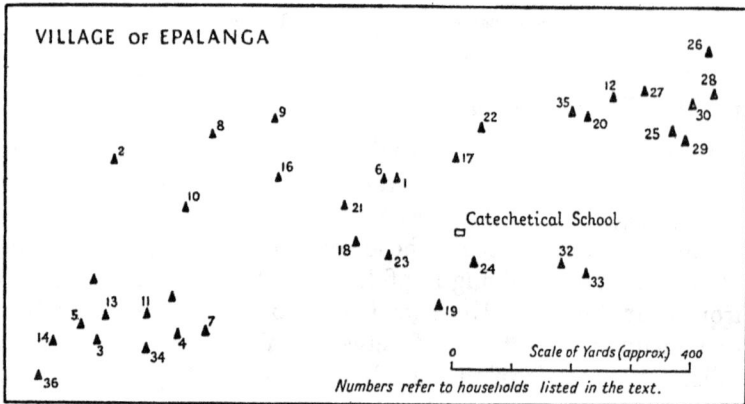

VILLAGE OF EPALANGA

Numbers refer to households listed in the text.

To some extent these differences of origin tended to be represented in the lay-out of the village. Sapapula's kin lived at the end of the village nearest the river, the kin of Mbati and Mwehombo lived in the centre of the village, and Ndjoleya's kinship core was to be found at the end of Epalanga by the Chicunda track. However, comparison of the list given below with the plan of the village show that the correspondence between core membership and the part of the village resided in is by no means total.[3]

In actual social life the differences between the cores to a large extent disappears. People from all cores take part in such activities as dances, funerals, house-building, and hunts, and this is facilitated by the numerous ties of kinship and marriage which exist between members of the different cores. Ndjoleya's

[3] Thus, Sendje, Sapapula's wife's mother, lived at Ndjoleya's end of the village. Ndjoleya had formerly lived at the other end of the village, but had moved. His 'sister', Tjingonene, still lived near his old home.

cluster was much more autonomous *vis-à-vis* Sapapula than were the members of the Mbati-Mwehombo grouping through the more numerous and closer kin ties; yet it would be wrong to regard Ndjoleya's kin as isolated.[4] This greater autonomy was a matter of degree rather than kind.

With regard to geographical origin, it is evident that the population had been recruited from over quite a wide area. Of the 36 household heads 7 were born in Cela of whom 6 had come from Cela to Gumba, and 1 had been born in Cela, then come to Gumba, then moved to Menga and then returned to Gumba. 3 household heads had come from Utende to Gumba, and 2 had come from Namba. 12 had come to Epalanga from Cassongue. 7 household heads (including 2 who had subsequently lived in Cassongue) had at one time lived in Katembo (the village associated with Mbati). 1 householder was apparently born in Gumba but had no Katembo link. 2 household heads were from Ndjandju (one having lived in Cassongue after leaving Ndjandju, the other being the catechist) and 1 was from Chicunda. On the origins of 5 household heads I have no information.

My information on Epalanga suffers from a number of gaps. Some genealogical information collected was lost. Too frequently I neglected to ask if a particular relationship was patrilateral or matrilateral, nor did I enquire sufficiently as to whether particular marriages were between kinsfolk or not.

These deficiencies to some extent 'fit' the kinship system. A kinship tie may exist between two people which is significant in the social relations between them, yet they may not be sure as to whether it is patrilateral or matrilateral, or even as to what is the category of kinship involved. Thus a resident of Simbwyikoka's village told me one day that Simbwyikoka was his 'brother', some time later he was a brother-in-law, and after this again said that he was a 'brother'.

There is also confusion over pedigrees. The pedigree which Simbwyikoka gave me in December 1955 differed from the one that he gave me in April 1956. Two people who claim to be

---

[4] Ndjoleya once referred to himself as *Osekulu yimbo* (elder of the *imbo*) this being a case of *imbo* used for a cluster within a village. Ndjoleya's folk recognized Sapapula as being head of the village.

'close' kin may not be able to indicate the set of genealogical[5] links between them and will not be at all surprised or even interested by this; hence it is impossible to draw up a genealogy of Epalanga. I have attempted to show the very complicated network of relationships by a series of charts—one big chart would have so many cross-cutting lines as to be largely unintelligible.

Three charts are given to illustrate particular sections of the mesh of kin and affinal ties. They are not intended as exhaustive records of the relationship of any one kinship core or of any single individual. Rather, they are intended to give a general impression of how the proliferation of the strands of kinship and marriage brings about a complicated and formless patchwork in which everybody is included.

2. *Information on Household Heads*

List I. Residents of Epalanga as of December 1956. Female household heads are indicated by a star against their names. The numbers are used on the map of the village (see p. 50).

Sapapula's Kinship Core

1. Aspirante, sister's son of Sapapula, son-in-law of Wayangu.
2. *Avilo, sister's daughter of Sapapula, 'sister' to Tjingonene (31).
3. Batista, son of Epalata (5) and husband of a sister of Kasosi (7).
4. Bernacio, son-in-law of Sapapula, 'son' to Kasosi (7).
5. Epalata, matrilateral cross-cousin of Sapapula.
6. Ernesto, sister's son of Sapapula, full brother of Aspirante (1) married to a daughter's daughter of Sasamela (see List II).
7. Kasosi, 'grandson' of Sapapula through being sister's son[6] to Wasuka (15). A 'son' to Guilherme and 'father' to Bernacio (4).

[5] Ovimbundu even traditionally seem to have been little interested in genealogies. (Information from Dr. G. M. Childs.)
[6] According to Umbundu kinship terminology, Wasuka being a matrilateral cross-cousin of Sapapula could call him 'father' and Kasosi could call his mother's brother's (Wasuka) father 'grandfather'.

8. *Natjingendele, cross-cousin of Sapapula, had formerly lived at the other end of Epalanga near her 'brother' Ndjoleya (30).
9. Patientia, 'brother' of Sapapula's wife Nahoka.
10. Sapapula, sister's son of Mbati, 'brother' of Luanga (21) and Mwehombo, not related to Ndjoleya (30) or Lusase.
11. Saviel, sister's son of Sapapula married to Soko, a daughter of Mwehombo. By an earlier marriage he had become affinally related to Tjingonene (31).
12. *Sendje, mother of Nahoka, Sapapula's wife.
13. Tjamwanga, matrilateral cross-cousin of Sapapula and paternal half-brother of Epalata (5).
14. Tjimbandongo, son of Epalata (5) and therefore a classificatory 'grandson' of Sapapula.
15. Wasuka, matrilateral cross-cousin of Sapapula, and 'brother' of Epalata (5).
16. *Wimbu, a widow, sister's daughter of Sapapula, her husband had been a mother's brother of Luanga (21).

The Mbati-Mwehombo kinship core

17. Armandio, sister's son of Mwehombo (and of Sapapula).
18. Gonçalve, own son of Mwehombo (therefore 'son' of Sapapula).
19. Jaime, son of Mbati—cross-cousin of Mwehombo, formerly married to Soko (daughter of Mwehombo) who was now the wife of Saviel (11), later married to Delfina, a brother's daughter of Ndjoleya.
20. Joaõ, cross-cousin of Sapapula. He tended, however, to be associated with the Mbati-Mwehombo kinship core, owing to his marriage to Paulina, daughter of Mwehombo, and full sister of Gonçalve (18).
21. Luanga, matrilateral 'brother' to Mwehombo (and also to Sapapula) patrilateral 'brother' to Ndjoleya. Luanga's wife Muhongo was a 'sister' of Maria, the wife of Paulo (24).
22. Manuel, sister's son of Mwehombo, his first wife had been a sister (not known if real or classificatory) of Maria, Paulo's wife (24).

23. *Nahenge, cross-cousin of Sapapula, and sister of João (20).
24. Paulo, 'elder of the catechetical school', sister's son of Mwehombo (and of Sapapula). His wife Maria was a daughter of Mbati.

Ndjoleya's kinship core

25. Augusto, sister's son to Ndjoleya, his wife Luisa was a daughter (by an earlier marriage) of Nalivonga, daughter of Sapapula and wife of Bernacio (4).
26. Costa, 'brother' of Ndjoleya (30), and husband of Nakalende, a cross-cousin of Paulo (24).
27. Cypriano, sister's son of Ndjoleya (30).
28. Ferreira, 'brother' of Ndjoleya (30).
29. Julio, sister's son of Ndjoleya and full brother of Augusto (25).
30. Ndjoleya, one of his wives was a sister (not known whether real or classificatory) of Bernacio, another a full sister of one of Mwehombo's wives.
31. *Tjingonene, 'sister' of Ndjoleya, by another path 'sister' of Avilo. Her daughter Feliciana was a cross-cousin of Nahoka, the wife of Sapapula, and had married Daniel, a sister's son of Lusase.

Persons with kin links to Lusase

32. Bartolomeu, sister's son of Lusase and also of Sapapula, 'son' of Wasuka (15), cross-cousin of Ndjoleya and also of Paulo (24).
33. *Nalundu, matrilateral 'sister' of Bartolomeu.

Other residents

34. *Nasemela, widow of Sasamela. (See List II).
35. Pedro Tjikete Santos, catechist.
36. *Tjambo, 'sister' of Bartolomeu (32), not included with him in the group linked to Lusase, since although she had formerly lived near his house, she moved to be near Tjimbandongo (14), whose 'mother' she was.

List II. Persons not living in Epalanga at the end of 1956, but significant for intra-village ties.

Angelo, son of Sasamela (q.v.) and therefore mother's brother to Teresa (wife of Ernesto (6) and daughter's daughter to Sasamela), had married Njamba, daughter (by another marriage) of Nakalende the wife of Costa (26).

Antonio Kasoma, patrilaterally a 'grandson' of Mbati had married three wives, one a daughter of Tjingonene (31), one a daughter of Sapapula, and one a sister's daughter of Guilherme. A 'brother' of his (not known if real or classificatory) had been an earlier husband of Nakalende, the wife of Costa (26). Kapapelo was a matrilateral cross-cousin of his.

Guilherme, sister's son of Kapapelo and Lusase, 'brother' to Bartolomeu (32) 'son' to Wasuka (15), 'father' to Kasosi (7) and 'grandson' to Sahuke.

Jeremias, Protestant catechist of Simbwyikoka village, wife's brother to Gonçalve (18), former husband of Natalia the sister of Aspirante (1) and Ernesto (6).

Kapapelo, 'brother' of Lusase, mother's brother of Bartolomeu (32) and Guilherme, patrilateral cross-cousin of Luanga (21), and matrilateral cross-cousin of Antonio Kasoma. Formerly married to the mother of Pungu, the fiancée of José the son of Paulo (24).

Lusase, chief of Gumba, 1954–1956, 'brother' to Kapapelo and Sahuke, mother's brother to Bartolomeu (32) and Guilherme. Another sister's son, Daniel of Kamupa, had married Feliciana, the daughter of Tjingonene (31), and cross-cousin of Nahoka the wife of Sapapula.

Pedro Nendi, son of Mbati and half-brother of Maria, wife of Paulo (24) and Jaime (19). His mother Wumba had after Mbati's death married Sahuke. Pedro Nendi lived in a hamlet just outside Epalanga. In it also lived his sister's son Cesario who was married to Natalia, a full sister of Aspirante (1) and Ernesto (6), and former wife of Jeremias (q.v.).

Sahuke, matrilateral 'brother' of Sapapula, and cross-cousin of Epalata (5). As noted he was a 'brother' of Lusase and a step-father to Pedro Nendi, also a 'brother' of Sasamela, a sister's son of Mbati and a mother's brother of Bartolomeu (32).

Sasamela, father of Angelo and grandfather of Teresa, the

wife of Ernesto (6). Patrilateral 'father' to Paula (24) and Saviel (11). Affinally related to Mwehombo, a 'sister' of whom he had married.

Wayangu, paternal half-brother of Mwehombo, resident at Epalanga till the end of 1955, wife's father to Aspirante (1) had married a sister (not clear whether own or classificatory) of Lusase.

3. *Kinship and marriage in the village setting*

The foregoing tabulated information and the charts indicate the two main principles of integration in Epalanga, as in other Umbundu villages, the settling of individuals near senior kinsmen and the existence of a number of intra-village marriage ties.

For a clearer outline of village structure to appear, it is necessary to give a brief sketch of the contemporary kinship system which will be discussed more thoroughly in later chapters. This is cognatic, with little distinction between patrilineal and matrilineal kin, the elementary family being the basic household unit, the individual being permitted to settle with any category of kin, and a high percentage of preferential marriages.[7]

The right of settling where one pleases, as 'the heart chooses', is recognized even in children. Minessi, the 7-year-old son of Gonçalve (18), used generally to eat at the household of his father's sister Paulina, the wife of João (20). Gonçalve said about this to me 'He is very fond of his father's sister.'

While the traditional norm by which a man lived in his father's village is still remembered, at least by older men, a

[7] Childs (p. 56) states that it is permitted to marry a cross-cousin on either side, a sister's daughter, and a father's sister. My informants generally agreed that the marriage with a father's sister was not and had not been permitted. Marriage is not permitted with 'true' kin of these categories. Padre Feltin, the superior of the Bimbe Catholic Mission who knew of the existence of these marriages, told me that very few Umbundu marriages came within the prohibited (a prohibition removable by a dispensation) degrees of kinship laid down by the Catholic Church (that is, up to, and including, third cousins). Such marriages in the past might have been with geographically as well as socially distant kin. Childs quotes a case of a marriage arranged, after the discovery of a kinship tie, between partners living as far apart as Ciyaka (Quiaca) and Ngalangi (Galangue).

father does not exercise great authority over his grown sons even if they live in the same village, nor does their living in different villages lead to a breach in personal relations. Sapapula who told me that a man should stay in his father's village till the latter's death had four sons, none of whom lived in Epalanga. Two lived in Menga (where Sapapula had lived up to 1946) and maintained friendly contact with their father. One who lived in Cela seemed socially as well as geographically more remote, and the fourth was a labour migrant given up for lost.

The preferential marriages[8] have continued in practice when most of the other institutions of the old kinship system have disintegrated. Their function is to multiply the relationships between individuals living in a particular neighbourhood, and to limit the socio-geographical range within which marriage partners are selected. Of a sample of 121 existing marriages 87, that is 70.3%, were with cross-cousins, and only 13.7% were with non-kinswomen.[9]

Even some of the non-kin marriages fitted into the general pattern of increasing ties within a limited social field. Thus in Epalanga Jaime (19) had married Delfina, a brother's daughter to Ndjoleya. They were not kinsfolk yet this fitted in with the pattern of kin marriages in increasing links between different kinship cores in the village. Similarly Costa (26) and his wife Nakalende were not agreed (when questioned separately) as to whether they were kinsfolk, but this is not really significant since

[8] I had been inclined to interpret these marriages as functions of the relations between kin groups. Dr. Mary Douglas has suggested to me that these marriages were in the past not related to any system of kin groups but had, as at the present day, the function of multiplying the kinship ties within a limited field. I do not know of any clear evidence which could at this time settle the point.

[9] I count here as kin marriages those between *vakwatjisoko*, funeral friends, who though not kinsfolk tend to be assimilated to cross-cousins in social usage. 'Cross-cousin' tends to be at the present time a blanket category, and I have repeatedly found asking men about their wife's kinship status that they would first give some other term and then change to 'cross-cousin'. [Epalume]. This explains why under present conditions the percentage of cross-cousin marriages in relation to the total number of marriages seems to be rising. Thus in 56 marriages (existing or terminated) contracted by 23 men who had taken part in the caravan trade, while the percentage of marriages with non-kinswomen was slightly smaller (12.5) the figure of marriages with cross-cousins was very much smaller (42.9) and the figure of marriages with kin other than cross-cousins, sister's daughters, and *vakwatjisoko* was much higher (25 %) compared to the contemporary figure of 5%.

their marriage also fits a general pattern of Umbundu marriage, a choice made within a limited range joining together individuals of different kinship cores.

The multiplication of ties and their concentration within a neighbourhood by this means do not prevent a man from having kin and affines a day or two's journey away. It has earlier been indicated that the population of Epalanga was from quite a wide area. Yet the consequences of previous preferential marriages (thus Paulo and Saviel were related both patrilaterally and matrilaterally) and the trend towards the establishment of new marriage ties had created a complicated mesh of linkages that has been described within a not particularly stable village population, whose senior residents had been there for only ten years. To use again the anthropological metaphor of kinship as a network, the network can have odd strings running out quite a way, but in a village the different ties will be bound up in a knot.

The long-range ties (with such obvious exceptions as those with kin living in cities) are not the result of the range of kin spreading wider and wider under modern conditions. The evidence of pedigrees indicates that kinship and marriage links between individuals in, and actual migration to and from Gumba and Cassongue, Cela, and Namba, date back well into the nineteenth century. There is far less evidence of connections and migration between Gumba and areas to the south and east. This geographical aspect of social relations persists at the present day.

It has been indicated that the high proportion of preferential marriages creates a certain local stability, since many marriages are with people living close to. Yet the basic stability lies not so much in the relative stability of a local population, but in the pattern by which links of distant kinship are changed into marriage ties and new bonds are speedily established among the fortuitously assembled population of a new village.

4. Headmen and Kinship Cores

I now turn to the other principle of village integration, the settling of individuals near senior kinsmen. In the previous chapter I have indicated that the position of headman is today a somewhat shadowy one, and that the headman emerges rather than succeeds by virtue of various grounds; the main ones being official recognition, some tie to the local chief, the presence of a core of one's kinsmen, a claim to be the first resident, and personality. During my stay Sapapula was as much a headman of Epalanga as anyone can reasonably be these days, yet his position had not always gone unchallenged.

In 1954 he had found himself in danger of being displaced by his matrilateral 'brother' Mwehombo. Both men, apparently, claimed that they had founded the village, both had substantial cores of kinsfolk in the village, and both possessed strong personalities. Sapapula by holding the ministerial title of Epalanga to Kafelo had had a stronger position in village affairs. This prop to his power was taken away when Kafelo was deposed from the chiefdom, and Luanga and Mwehombo purchased the title of Epalanga from Lusase.

In this partnership Mwehombo must have been the leading personality, Luanga being extremely amiable but not at all domineering or energetic. Mwehombo's idea was presumably to establish himself as recognized headman of Epalanga, and to obtain whatever advantages were to be gained from an association with Lusase. Luanga's aim, from what he told me, was to escape contract labour by having a position as a traditional headman and title-holder. Titles will still be sought after, although the substance of power has gone, so long as they can confer some prestige or protection from administrative labour demands. It was not customary for the role of Epalanga to be held by two people jointly.

Mwehombo died shortly after this. He had been baptized by the name of Simon when dying on January 13th 1955, when his social personality began its posthumous career. At the inquest, which was held according to the old Umbundu pattern in which the corpse suspended in a hammock from a pole held by two men was supposed to answer questions by the way it swung, it was found that Mwehombo had suffered the proverbial fate of the sorcerer in being killed by the spirit he had used to kill others.

The role of the questioner was taken by Paulo, sister's son to

Mwehombo, and elder of the school, a post he would certainly have lost had this come to the ears of the missionaries. Attitudes to the verdict are interesting. Sapapula assured me that Mwehombo had killed many people by sorcery both sons and sisters' sons; Luanga did not see the contradiction which I pointed out to him of his saying both that Mwehombo was good and that he had practised sorcery; Gonçalve, Mwehombo's son, appeared sceptical of the verdict, as did Aspirante, Sapapula's sister's son who was married to a daughter of Mwehombo's half-brother, Wayangu.

The verdict did not prevent Mwehombo having an impressive funeral. He was buried according to his wishes in the traditional hammock placed in the circular grave, instead of the modern coffin placed in the modern oblong grave. As a caravan-leader he was buried by the track to Chicunda at the point where the path to Epalanga branched off. A low thatched covering was erected over his grave with the horns of the beast killed at the funeral on it. In 1956 Gonçalve and Pedro Nendi, son of Mbati and therefore a cross-cousin of Mwehombo, replaced this by a concrete memorial in the form of a cross with the base inscribed in Portuguese 'Simon Mwehombo Native of Gumba Great Man died 13th January 1955.'

Thus Mwehombo had twice undergone conversion from pagan to Christian, once as he lay dying and once after death. His posthumous conviction for sorcery affected neither the form of funeral, nor the continued residence of his kin in the village. His conviction for sorcery was a reflection of the social strains in which he had been involved, not the opening of another cycle of conflict. The kinship cores are not segments opposing one another as in a lineage system; they possess no clearly defined boundaries[10] or continuing existence in time. Their existence is dependent on the persons around whom the cores have formed, and on their deaths they lack any integrating principles. Mwehombo dead, his kinsfolk mostly found no objection in continuing to live in the village where his rival now lived as undisputed traditional headman.

There is no word in Umbundu for these groupings. The

[10] For example I have included Joaõ in the Mwehombo-Mbati kinship core, on the basis of association, but he came to the village through a tie with Sapapula.

word 'otjitawila' is given by Dr. Childs[11] as being used for a section of the village; however, I have not found this word known locally.

It may be asked how typical Epalanga is of other villages. In size it is larger than usual, having 36 households. (The average number, using figures from 14 villages, is 18.36 households; the largest, Epalanga, had 36 and the smallest 5.) In structure other villages presented the same picture of ill-defined kinship cores held together by a network of kin and affinal ties, with village headmen emerging by a varying collection of claims, of which the most significant seemed to be a position as the principal focus of kinship ties.

5. *Kinsmen and the Choice of Residence*

When one asks a man why he has settled in a particular village, a common enough answer is that he has settled there because he has 'family' there. When asked who his 'family' (the Portuguese word *família* is used even by non-Portuguese speakers) is, he will give the name of a senior kinsman, or he may give more than one name. He may even give the name of somebody living outside the village. Thus in Epalanga when I asked Bartolomeu why he had settled there he replied that it was because of his mother's brother Lusase who was not an Epalanga resident. It was therefore not practicable for me, as I had at one time intended, to find which categories of kin are most likely to be settled with, by asking individuals in villages I censused, and obtaining percentages.

It is possible to indicate some of the 'pulls' which affect a choice of residence. In the traditional system, when a boy's father died he would settle with a father's brother. Nowadays, it is generally expected that he will settle with his mother's brother, this being the answer given by informants when asked where he will go. In practice, the pull of the mother's brother's household for a child does not seem to be so strong. In Epalanga, out of thirteen persons under 20 who had neither father nor mother resident in the village, only one was living with a mother's brother.

[11] See Childs, pp. 36–37.

On the village level, however, the importance of the mother's brother tie and of the tie between matrilateral 'brothers' becomes very apparent. None of Sapapula's four sons had settled in Epalanga, and his only classificatory 'son' was Gonçalve, own son to Mwehombo, Sapapula's matrilateral 'brother'. Seven household heads were sister's sons of Sapapula. This trend for matrilateral ties to predominate is marked also in Katembo and Mbunga, but less evident at Belem. Indeed, 'neo-matrilinearity' as a principle of village structure may be a general and not simply a local feature of Umbundu society, since Mr. C. M. N. White[12] has found that the settlements of Ovimbundu within Northern Rhodesia are marked by a predominance of matrilateral ties. This is referable to the contemporary kinship system in which the father-son tie is predominantly a personal one, with a limited extension of attitudes to classificatory fathers, whereas a man's relation with a mother's brother seems little affected by the question of genealogical distance. Perhaps the relations between the group of agnatic kin were so closely tied to the old village structure that when it broke up it disintegrated also the wider agnatic ties. Yet at the same time such matrilineal institutions as matrilineal inheritance and the non-repayment of loans among matrikin have weakened or disappeared.

Running counter to this principle of settling in the village of a senior kinsman who is likely to belong to one's matrikin, is the principle of cross-cousin marriage. 'If you have married your cross-cousin when your son grows up he will see a cross-cousin here, a cross-cousin there, and so he will stay.' That is, a man will stay in his father's village not simply by virtue of the father-son tie but because he will be surrounded by kinsmen. The relation between cross-cousins is one of equality and solidarity, expressed in joking and in burial services. To say that one stays in a place because one has cross-cousins at hand is to indicate an ideal of equal relations with a circle of kinsmen rather than attachment to the following of an important kinsman.

These two principles co-exist in actual social life. A man will recognize and respect a number of senior kinsmen living in his

[12] In letters.

neighbourhood and will explain his choice of residence by quoting the names of one or more of these; yet the weaving together of so many strands of kinship and affinity, ultimately through marriage links, is what gives the local population its relative degree of stability. It should be emphasized that the integration established within a village by the network of kinship and affinal ties is dependent on the integration created by the same amorphous network which runs through and beyond the sub-chiefdom. It is this network into which the individual is woven by multiple ties that absorbs the neo-matrilineal pull apparent to some degree in choice of residence and keeps the system essentially cognatic.

The use of the word *família* reflects this situation. A man may say of a particular senior kinsman 'He is my *família*', that is, my kinsman, my most important kinsman with whom I have settled, yet also he may say 'My *família* is in Cela', that is, the greater part of my kinsmen live in Cela. When Bartolomeu explained that he had settled where he did because of Lusase, he was perhaps combining the two kinds of references. He had settled in Gumba because he had a large number of kinsmen there among whom Lusase was pre-eminent. A man explaining the locality of his *família* in the wider sense will associate it with a particular sub-chiefdom—'My family is all in Menga'—when he is outside it; when he is in it he is more likely to refer to a particular village.

Although individuals living in a village may have come there through several kinship sources yet the majority of them will probably have some kinship or affinal tie with the traditional headman. This collection of individual ties does not provide the headman with a body of followers, nor is having a large number of dependants a value of contemporary Umbundu culture. If it were felt that the best thing to be in life is the patron of a body of kinsmen and followers, headmanship would survive as a predominant influence in local life despite the collapse of its political and legal responsibilities. In fact not even old men feel this way.

The idea of the village as a corporate group with a jural and political personality rather than a residential unit has not survived the break-up of agnatic solidarity, the disappearance of the men's house, and the headman's loss of status. The new institution of the catechetical school does not revive village solidarity in this form. The contemporary Ovimbundu do not live in a 'village headman society' comparable to those of British Central Africa,[13] since the concept and manifestations of village solidarity around a headman are so notably deficient. Reference may also be made to the economic ethics of the Ovimbundu with their approval of making money and the belief that all loans even within the circle of the elementary family should be repaid, that is, wealth is seen by all as an end in itself rather than a means of obtaining personal loyalties.

In the previous chapter it was shown how the traditional headmanship is no longer a significant legal and political institution. In this chapter I have tried to indicate that it lacks sources of authority and prestige within the village.

The line of argument has involved reference to the contemporary kinship system of which an outline has been given. This will be more fully discussed in later chapters, when a more detailed comparison of present institutions with the traditional kinship system will be made.

[13] For an example of these societies see J. C. Mitchell, *The Yao Village*, Manchester 1956.

CHAPTER V

VILLAGE ECONOMICS

———◆◆◆◆◆/◉/◆◆◆◆◆◆———

The homeland of the Ovimbundu, the Benguela Highland, is mostly over 4,000 feet above sea-level. Rainfall is 50–60 inches a year, and the rainy season is from September to April.[1] In this season after a downpour there is frequently a cooling of the air, and the most intense heat comes just before the rainy season, during the dry spell that occurs in or about February, and just after the rains. Between the middle of May and the middle of July the nights and early mornings are bitterly cold but the days are pleasantly cool. After the middle of July the temperature gradually rises.

The soil of the Highland is poor; the Ovimbundu industriously cultivate beans, manioc, maize, potatoes, and tobacco. Less frequently they have coffee plants, fruit trees, and sisal. Occasionally wheat is grown but the ground is not really suitable. I am told that rice could be grown in the stream valleys. Four field types are recognized by the Ovimbundu—*otjumbo* (garden), *onaka* (stream-valley garden), *ombanda* (in ground sloping up from a stream), and *epya* (a field away from the streams on level ground).[2]

Umbundu country is well supplied with water in streams and rivers, and the Ovimbundu have built irrigation channels wherever possible. Cultivation in the stream valleys, that is, of the *onaka* type of garden, has only been practised since the 1870's or 80's.[3] They are planted in August or the beginning of September, and give crops in December and January. The

---

[1] For an excellent account of Umbundu habitat see Childs, pp. 1–11.

[2] Albino Alves, *Dicionário Etimologico Bundo-Português*, Lisbon, 1951, Vol. I, p. 659 gives ombanda as a synonym of onaka.

[3] Private information.

maize from these beds is for home consumption, and it comes at a time when maize supplies are running low, and some people have to rely on manioc. The *ombanda* type is sown in September and early October. Then the main fields (*ovapya*, plural of *epya*) are sown in October and November, and only after this is maize sown in the gardens round the houses. In December and January the people are busy hoeing the fields and in February the sowing of beans takes place, continuing into March. This is followed by the harvesting of the gardens in the village, and by the gathering of the maize in the fields, the maize then being placed in field huts to dry. This takes place in March and April, and with its ending the dry season has come.

The dry season is the time for travelling to see relatives and for getting married, since the burden of work is much reduced. May is a good time to clear the bush and then and in later months there is time to build houses. During the dry season there was much more chance of finding people at home, and there were far more festive occasions. This is also a time when men and women can practise crafts such as basketry, fish-trap making, pottery, and so on. In July, the maize dried in the field hut is pounded and brought back to the village, whence it is taken to the traders for sale. The pounding and carrying is often the work of parties of friends and relatives who are rewarded with beer. Occasionally somebody's maize is collected like this well into September, but most people finish in August. By August the grass has grown very high, and the firing of it is the beginning of large-scale hunts in which men and boys from several villages may join together. Hunts may be undertaken by individuals or by groups at other times of the year either as a hobby or to kill a destructive wild pig (in which case the hunt will be undertaken by a group of people). September is a good month for fishing. The fire has cleared the stream valleys which can now be sown, thus starting off the year's cycle again.

There is no shortage of land, and hence questions of land rights seldom come up in social relations. A village headman has no rights over land outside his village, and even within a village there are strips of bush from which a new garden can be cut. Land is very occasionally sold. For instance a man return-

ing home from labour in October wants cleared fields to sow.
If he cannot find any kinsman who would give him a cleared
field he will have to buy one, and will have perhaps to pay 200
escudos (£2 10s.). A man retains his rights to fields in a village
he no longer inhabits.

The Ovimbundu keep cattle, sheep, goats, pigs, and fowls.
The cattle are not milked but are used in sacrifices, and for
fines; some have been brought by Ovimbundu from Kwanyama Ambo country but they do not seem to thrive in this
neighbourhood. Sheep are few. In my village goats were much
less numerous than chickens or pigs. The traders and European
residents buy cattle, chickens, and pigs.

Fishing and hunting are practised, but despite the ingenious
fish-traps, nets, poisons and weirs used for the first, and the
popular enthusiasm for, and ritual associations of the second,
neither dominates the actual food supply and ecological background in the way that maize does.

The Ovimbundu believe that the dry-season grass fires also
help to fertilize the soil by leaving ashes. Ashes are sometimes
spread in a village garden, and dry grass may also be left in a
field for this purpose. Soil beside trees is considered to be especially rich, as to some extent are the sites of former villages.
There is no idea of crop rotation and a field is worked for as long
as it is fertile, that is indefinitely for an *onaka* and from three to
six years, sometimes more, for a field of the *epya* type. The hoe
is still the standard means of cultivation and the plough is a
rarity.

Coffee-growing on any scale is usually undertaken by people
living away from the villages, except for the Protestants who
have been encouraged by their missionaries to plant coffee in
their villages. Coffee, like maize, is bought by the traders.
However, at least two local coffee-growers sold their coffee at
Porto Amboim on the coast to get a better price. Basically, the
agricultural economy of the neighbourhood is based on maize,
grown by methods of shifting cultivation. The frequency with
which villages rise and fall and individuals change from one
village to another is entirely consistent with this type of agriculture.

Axe and hoe blades, blankets, cloths, clothing, cutlery,

67

drinking-mugs, lanterns, metal plates, pens, pencils, wine, and writing slates are bought from the traders. Axe and hoe handles, buckets, bedsteads, beer, bows and arrows, chairs, fish-traps, mats, mush sticks, pottery, pounding-blocks, stools, tables, and small metal objects such as knives are made by Ovimbundu and may be sold locally. To this local trade may be added the selling of pieces of meat by anyone who has killed a pig, or gone hunting and killed a duiker. Very occasionally somebody who has bought cloths in a town or has some hand-made object superior to the local average may tour villages selling his goods as a pedlar.

The only trade which at all recalls the days of the caravan trade is the cattle trade with the Kwanyama Ambo. As in the rubber trade the Ovimbundu make use of their intermediary geographical position. They obtain from Luanda shells called *olomande* (singular *omande*). One of these shells costs 10 escudos (2s. 6d.) at Luanda and ten of them will buy a beast in Kwanyama country. Alternatively 30 rounds of tobacco will buy a beast there. I knew several men who had made, or planned to make, trips of this nature. The analogy with the caravan trade breaks down, however, when the relative importance of the two is examined. The caravan trade determined the economic standards of the Ovimbundu, absorbed a great part of the time of every able-bodied man and youth, and influenced every aspect of Umbundu life from the foreign policy of the kings to accusations of sorcery; the cattle-keeping is relatively unimportant economically since the Ovimbundu do not drink milk, and eat meat, even chicken or pork, very irregularly, nor does the occasional sale of cattle to traders altogether balance their uncertain survival away from their indigenous grasses. The real importance of cattle in the economy seems to be as a form of capital investment for spare savings, an investment which can be liquidated either by sacrifice on ceremonial occasions or back into money by sale. Socially, it may be thought of as marking the survival of the Umbundu capacity and enthusiasm for trading in an age when the economic situation has closed the old routes. Indeed, perhaps the sub-conscious motive for the Ovimbundu who trade is to show that they can act outside of that economic framework of cultivation and wage labour which I have described as affecting the Ovimbundu as a whole.

It is not easy to compose budgets of household expenditure and income, partly because they have not yet much of a 'book-keeping' outlook, and partly because they suspect the motives behind questions of this sort. My own opinion is that from agriculture the average household would earn considerably less than 1,000 escudos (£12. 10s.) a year. The Banco de Angola in its Report for 1955[4] gives a budget for an African family at Silva Porto, consisting of father, mother, and two young children, having agriculture as their only source of income. Their total yearly income is given as 7,750 escudos (about £96. 17s. 6d.). Even allowing for the higher prices paid for crops on the railway line, an income of this order is far above anything earned by the average cultivating household, though it might be earned by the few men who cultivated coffee extensively and lived in Portuguese style.

Some details of the economic life of individuals may give depth to this chapter. Kambungo, a kinsman of Sapapula living in Menga, was a man of over sixty who had in his youth travelled on the caravans. He had a large house but lived in a village amongst kinsfolk. In June 1955 he had been in Kwanyama country where, with shells obtained at Luanda, he had bought cattle and for 15 of the *olomande* shells he got a sewing-machine. In the year 1955–6 (very roughly from the end of the dry season in '55 to the same period in '56) he had sold ten sacks of maize at 25 escudos each and six sacks of beans for 60 escudos each. He had, however, concluded that maize did not pay and had started to grow coffee. He had sold one beast for 900 escudos (£10. 15. 0), and had also sold ten sheep for 100 escudos (£1. 5. 0) each. He had also sold a coat for 120 escudos (£1. 10. 0).

The principal item of Kambungo's expenditure was a bicycle which he bought for 1,500 escudos (£18. 15s.). He had also bought two beds each 100 escudos, and ten plates 100 escudos altogether. He had bought ten bottles of wine, at 5 escudos each, and had also bought some indigenous rum, price not noted. Ten traditional sleeping mats cost 2½ escudos each, and four

[4] Quoted by Egerton, pp. 124–5.

pairs of shorts cost 70 escudos each. Two kerchiefs for women cost 50 escudos each.

Total income recorded is 2,870 escudos (£35. 17. 6). Total expenditure recorded is 2,255 escudos (£28. 3. 9). It should be noted that Kambungo, while not living in Portuguese style, was considered wealthy for an Otjimbundu and that much of his income, for instance from the sale of the ten sheep, was from exceptional sales which could not be annually repeated. As regards livestock Kambungo had five head of cattle, five chickens, four sheep and two ducks.

More typical would be the year's expenditure of Pedro Musungu, an inhabitant of a Protestant village, who had bought two cloths, each of four metres and each costing 50 escudos (about 12s 6d.) for his wife, and for each of his four children two cloths, one 25 escudos the other 30. He had bought a hoe for 7½ escudos, a book for the same. To this total expenditure should be added the tax (180 escudos) plus the communal fines levied each year for burning the grass and so on which may come to 40 escudos or more. The total expenditure then would be about 555 escudos (£6. 18. 9). It was not possible to calculate his income since he could not remember how many sacks he had sold to the traders. He had, however, raised 200 escudos by selling a pig and had got 40 escudos for two kilos of coffee, though most of the coffee he planted had not produced berries.

A yet poorer household was that of Cypriano, a villager of Epalanga with a wife and two young children. His maize crop in 1956 had gone to pay debts to traders, for the 1955 maize harvest had been very poor. He had got tax-money by making pounding-blocks, and pounding-sticks (for beating out maize), but could not remember how much he had earned thus. Although Cypriano's stock amounted to one sow and one hen, he and his wife had a set of smart clothes for special occasions, like all Ovimbundu.

Much better off was Luveli, who like Cypriano combined a craft with agriculture. He had sold ten kilos of coffee for 20 escudos each, as well as twelve sacks of maize at 25 escudos each and two sacks of potatoes at 20 escudos each, making a total agricultural revenue of 540 escudos, to which must be added

Luveli's income from bricklaying. The laying of the bricks that form a modern villager's house may bring 100 escudos.

The basic cash need of an Otjimbundu, then, is for money to pay government demands and to provide clothing for his wife and children, who seem more likely than the men to get new clothing every year.[5] Add to this the possibility of other calls (e.g. provision for a relative's funeral) a desirable income even for this low level of consumption would be 400 escudos (£5) and a more prosperous villager might earn and spend double the amount. Exceptional individuals still remaining within the normal conditions of Umbundu cultural and social life, such as Kambungo, may earn from 2,000 to 3,000 escudos a year, perhaps even more, from agriculture. Maize is the foundation of the agricultural economy, but Kambungo's remark that maize did not pay seems to reflect a trend to find other openings such as growing coffee, which is, however, subject to difficulties of climate.

Within the villages there is some trade in handmade objects such as pottery, sleeping-mats, and sticks for stirring mush, and there are quite a number of bricklayers, carpenters, and tailors (proprietors of sewing-machines) who have acquired European skills which bring them money. These craftsmen are, on payment of a fee of 250 escudos (a figure given me by a tailor), exempt from contract labour.

Many European residents seem to think that the only European products natives desire are cloths, clothing, and wine. This is not so; villagers wanted me to sell them kerosene for lamps, D.D.T. powder for their hair, and soap. It is interesting that the occasions on which an Otjimbundu would accumulate large (for him) sums all fall outside the maize-for-cloth pattern of trading. These occasions are bridewealth payment (and counting all expenses this may well come to 800 escudos—£10 or more), which is a traditional due, the purchase of bicycles (according to place of purchase from 1,200 escudos [£15] to 1,500 escudos [£18. 15. 0]) which are prestige-giving objects, and the trading journeys to buy cattle. Kambungo had

[5] The trader whose opinions I have previously quoted (Senhor Alberto Oliveira Mendes of Chicunda), remarked, 'It is the women who save us. The men make a shirt last for three or four years but the women get something new every year.'

71

spent 10,000 escudos, he told me, in buying shells to trade in Kwanyama country and even if this be regarded as an exaggeration such an expedition will cost at least several hundred escudos.

I have not so far discussed labour migration and its economic consequences. There are three ways of going out to work: being recruited for 'contract labour', which involves selection by the chief and government headmen who send people to the post whence they are directed to wherever they are required; being recruited by labour-recruiters who visit villages with their lorries; and travelling, usually on foot, to find work. Contract labour is for a year, which may be followed by a fortnight's work at the post to which the *contratados* are returned. The coffee plantations of Amboim and Seles are important centres for voluntary labour from Gumba and neighbouring chiefdoms. Women, and boys from ten years up, go to work there for spells which may be only two months. However, even in Gumba whose people have a reputation for backwardness and for lack of enthusiasm for going away to work, there is nothing at all surprising in meeting men who have learnt a few words of English in Johannesburg.

Of the 36 household heads of Epalanga, 9 were women, and 8 were men who for one reason or another (elders, cripples, the catechist) would not leave the village. Of the other 19, 6 were absent as labourers during some part of my stay, and this figure excludes individuals who were not expected home within a year. In the cities there are large numbers of permanently or semi-permanently urbanized Ovimbundu, who have largely lost contact with their home villages. Some people who have spent years in the towns may come home—in Epalanga there were at least five women who had visited cities.

Although almost all able-bodied men and many women have lived outside the context of village life as servants to Europeans, as labourers on plantations, and as urban workers, it would be a mistake to think of the rural areas of the Benguela Highland, as being labour reservoirs economically dependent on the towns. It seems that prices of manufactured goods are lower near the railway line and in the cities; hence a man returning from wage labour may buy cloths, a bicycle, a sewing-machine, or a gramophone in a town rather than at a trader's near his home village. Most of the money paid for purchases at the stores is money raised by selling crops or livestock. Through labour migration there is, however, some transmission of skills; it is easy to find bricklayers and carpenters of a sort even in Gumba.

Money, rather than barter, is the principal means of exchange among the villages in the selling of local products, and even of meat from pigs. Payment for labour service, such as assistance in house-building and in bringing in maize, is made in beer, except among Protestants who substitute a meal. There is also a custom by which a household which finds, probably at the end of the dry season, that it has not enough maize will make beer to exchange on a particular day for maize.

Ties of kinship and friendship have some economic significance. A kinsman will help with house-building without expecting payment; likewise a man who has a cleared field which he does not want to use may sell it for 200 escudos (£2. 10s.) but would give it free to a kinsman. A man may make a charge for lending his bicycle, though this varies with individuals; he certainly would not do so if it were lent to a friend. Loans between kinsmen should be repaid, and a tailor with a sewing-machine will make the same charges to relatives as to non-kinsmen.

There are few occasions for groups to work together. The unit of consumption and production is the domestic family. Even here, the husband, each wife, and the adolescents have their own fields, though a man may help his wife. Such other occasions of mutual help, in clearing a field, which may occur between friends or kinsmen, will only bring a few, often only two of them.

The Ovimbundu I knew were (with exceptions) not avaricious or grasping; thus, beer might be given to people who have not actually worked in house-building parties. It is regarded as a moral duty to pay one's monetary debts as soon as possible. On various occasions I lent money to people who were pressed and I received back all the money lent. Borrowers insisted that borrowings should be written down, and that the paper on which it was written should be given to them when they paid, or destroyed. Making money and being rich are regarded with unambiguous approval, though there is a certain undertone suggesting cunning in the verb *oku lunguka* (to be shrewd) used about prosperous people. The old suspicion of sorcery attaching to people who were more successful farmers than their neighbours[6] seems to have disappeared. While a prosperous villager would be expected to lend money to a poorer kinsman (provided the latter was not known as a bad debtor) yet, the situation which occurs in other parts of Africa, where, as Dr. V. W. Turner notes of the Mwinilunga Ndembu, prosperous Africans 'find themselves increasingly embarrassed by the demands of their kin for presents in cash and kind'[7], would not arise among the Ovimbundu, who would regard such demands as being unjustified, even outrageous.

Wealthy Ovimbundu may spend some of their wealth on clothing and on drink. Cattle-buying has been noted as a form of capital investment and the same term may be used of small stock buying. Another way of disposing of money is by building a house of bricks with the assistance of a bricklayer. A plough may be, but rarely is, bought by two men joining together to pool their money. Generally speaking, the agricultural technology of the Ovimbundu has been little changed since 1911 except for the spread of the techniques of coffee-growing.

It has been noted earlier that the Ovimbundu play an important part in the economic life of Angola both as cultivators and labourers. In this chapter an attempt has been made to show how at the local level it is the cultivation of cash crops, rather than migration for wage labour, which incorporates villagers into the commercial economy of modern Angola. The main source of money in rural areas is the trader's store, which is also the main recipient of money, apart from the administration. While trade both between Ovimbundu and between Ovimbundu and other tribes survives on a minor scale, the social institutions associated with the rubber trade, the large caravans, the non-repayable loans within the matrilineal group, and the obligations of wealthy traders to assist their kin, have disappeared. The contemporary social structure with the

---

[6] Childs, pp. 106–8.

[7] V. W. Turner, op. cit., p. 135.

instability of village sites and village populations, the marked emergence of the elementary family, and the non-existence of economic activities and rights associated with corporate groups, is consistent with the growth of cash crops by shifting cultivation.

CHAPTER VI

THE CATECHETICAL SCHOOL

——————◦◦◦◦◦◦◦◦◦◦————————

Both the Catholic and Protestant missions have, in order to provide religious teaching and leadership at the village level, made use of catechists whose responsibility it is to prepare people for baptism and children for Communion by teaching them catechism, to lead the village people in prayers, and to maintain contact with the missions. There are a number of differences between the roles of the Catholic and the Protestant catechists. As most of the Christians in my immediate neighbourhood were Catholics, I shall deal in this chapter with the Catholic catechists, though I shall indicate some of the differences which the Protestant organization shows.

In the early days large numbers of Christians settled round the missions. The first Catholic converts were slaves purchased from traders by the missionaries and settled in villages near the missions. While the Protestant missions did not do this, they were somewhat embarrassed by the large crowds of converts who settled round mission stations.[1] The missions expanded by sending out catechists who gathered converts. At one time the practice was for the Christians to settle in a 'school village', which was in fact a hamlet partially separated from the rest of the village from which its membership was recruited. This is still found in some Gumba villages. In other villages, however, there is no geographical division between Christian and pagan, and the school may occupy a central position in the lay-out of the village. There are as yet no purely Catholic villages in Gumba. These are established by the missionaries when there is considered to be a significant number of Catholic married couples. This pattern is followed even on the outskirts of Nova Lisboa.

[1] Childs, p. 66.

76

The catechist is appointed by the mission, though there is a fairly common tendency for him to have relatives in the village where he is catechist. It is often the case that somebody who is already recognized by the mission as qualified to be a catechist, that is, has a good knowledge of the catechism, prayers and hymns, may be asked by some kinsman to come to his village to teach catechism, and his acceptance needs only to be confirmed by the mission. Even in Gumba, notable for the relative strength of its surviving paganism and the relatively slow rate of conversion, every village except the chief's capital and the hamlets had a catechetical school.

The catechist does not receive a salary from the mission. He is, however, exempt from the personal tax, and is not liable for road-work or contract labour. He may be able to persuade his flock to cultivate a field for him, and the school itself, and perhaps a house for visiting missionaries, will be built by the school people. The other representative of the school is the elder of the school, whose responsibility is to arrange for the catechist's settling down in the village, and his getting on well with the local people. This office had particular importance in the days when a catechist might be sent from the mission to a region quite different from his own. Nowadays, when so many catechists have kin in the villages where they settle, the balance of influence between catechist and elder of the school will depend on their personalities. In one village the elder of the school may be pushing and shrewd, and the catechist may be rather under his influence; in another an active, enterprising, catechist may make the elder of the school his assistant. The elder of the school is not exempt from taxes, but is not called on for labour service.

The school people may include both baptized people and catechumens. For both the word *vakwasikola* (they of the school) applies and the former may be called Christians, and these will sometimes object to non-baptized people using Christian names. The period of catechumenate is three years, but people who learn catechism quickly are given baptism in two years. There are a certain number of peripheral school people who may turn up at the school for prayers but who are not actively learning the catechism. There are other people who do not

77

usually come to the school but say they want to be baptized. Many people who would have to be classified as pagans are people with Christian names who at one time attended catechism classes and prayers, and who may very occasionally turn up to some service, for instance the Corpus Christi procession at the Mission.

Adult and adolescent converts may only receive baptism at the mission. The children of Christian parents are baptized by priests on their visits to the villages; it is the catechists' duty to teach them catechism in preparation for their first confession and communion which should take place when they are about seven to ten years old. The missionaries frequently complain of the inadequacies of the catechists as teachers of doctrine. Few of the old pupils of the elementary school at the Bimbe mission become catechists, as there is no pay attached to it. Some, certainly, of the catechists are devoted and intelligent men, and a few have a real gift for speaking in public.

Some catechists attempt to teach their pupils the three Rs; and a catechist ready to teach reading, writing and counting will find a number of boys eager to learn. There are about half a dozen 'rudimentary', that is pre-primary, schools dependent on the Bimbe mission, none of which is in Gumba or Chicunda, and a primary school at the mission itself. Learning to read and write is not confined to Christians; some pagans in Epalanga could write their names, and I was told that among contract labourers on plantations those who were literate would teach those who were not in the dormitories at night.

Apart from religious instruction, the catechists have the duty of leading the people in morning and evening prayers at the school. These prayers are in Umbundu with occasionally a hymn in Portuguese. On Sunday mornings there is a longer set of prayers and hymns, some in Latin taken from the Mass, held about ten o'clock. Only a few people turn up for morning prayers, considerably more to evening prayers, and nearly everybody who can be considered a 'school person' comes to the Sunday gathering.

The evening gatherings for prayers may be used as opportunities for announcing news—e.g. the approaching visit of a missionary. More usually they are followed and sometimes preceded by singing, and dancing. There are a certain number of 'school' songs as distinct from hymns, which are semi- or non-religious in nature, which are taught by the catechist and are sung on these occasions with other Umbundu traditional songs. There seems to be little composition of songs by present day Ovimbundu nor do they know popular Portuguese songs.

The school itself, the centre of these activities, is generally built of adobe bricks in the shape of a church. In any village where there is a fair number of school people it will be the largest building in the village and even in villages of mixed Christian and pagan population the school building tends to be in the centre of the village, a topographical reflection of the social significance of the catechist and the catechetical school. In the school men and women are separated, men on the right, women on the left, a custom also found in some Angolan parish churches.

The catechist's presence is a mark of the identity of the village. The catechetical school is the only institution which groups people of different domestic groups on a village-wide basis, and in which people participate in a wider set of social relations on a village and not on an individual basis, as people are linked to kinsmen, or to the post or to an employer. One can and does associate oneself with a village if one does not belong geographically to it but simply attends its school. Thus Fernando considered himself as belonging to the village of Ngolo Catolica whose catechetical school he attended, although his house was well away from the main village, being much nearer the Protestant village of Vila Graça, where indeed he had kinsmen. When I asked a woman where she lived she replied by giving the name of the village catechist. The only occasions on which a group of people represent one village vis-à-vis another are in connection with the travels of missionaries, and in the wedding feasts, which will be described in another chapter.

A missionary on leaving one village for another has his luggage carried by the school people of the village where he has been staying, who will march singing, with perhaps a boy banging on a drum. When they get to the next village they will be greeted at the entrance into the village by the catechist and his people, who will be neatly dressed and lined up. The welcoming catechist will deliver a speech in Portuguese, and will conclude with three Vivas one, say, for the Bishop of Nova Lisboa, one for the Mission, and one for the visiting priest. These may be varied—I have heard a Viva for Diogo Cão, the Portuguese navigator who discovered Angola. This formal welcome to a procession seems copied from the welcome given to the party from the bride's village when they arrive at the bridegroom's village; and this welcome has in turn copied elements—speeches in Portuguese and calls for Vivas—from the reception of missionaries. Then both parties singing and dancing will proceed to the house where the priest is to stay. The people of the welcoming village should have taken over his luggage at the point where they met his party—if they have not, his carriers will complain vigorously.

It is the catechist's responsibility to get his people to provide the customary gifts of a chicken or two, and possibly eggs and bananas to the visiting priest. He must explain the spiritual state of the school people to the missionary, notably telling him if any of the Christians have married according to pagan custom. It is to him that the priest will direct criticisms on the state of the school building or on the lack of catechetical knowledge of the people. The catechist has also the obligation to visit the mission occasionally during the year—how often depends on nearness, on circumstances and on his own enthusiasm. The most popular times for visiting the mission are Christmastime, the New Year, Easter, and Corpus Christi, when the catechist may go with a number of the school people, though individual Christians also go alone. A catechist will also visit the mission when he has some catechumens who are sufficiently advanced to be tested on their religious knowledge. He has also a general responsibility to report to the mission the activities of diviners, or Christians who have married polygamously. He may also be responsible for referring other disputes to the mission, or for obtaining a letter of commendation to the post in some dispute.

The catechist, then, does not have much authority of his own; his personal role is that of a teacher and leader of prayers. He can, however, invoke the authority of the mission, which even in non-religious matters has influence with the post, and can through this influence effect the arrest of diviners and baptized polygamists, or intervene on the side of somebody called before the post.

A catechist may be removed from his position by the mission for incompetence, or for moral failings, such as unchastity or rum-brewing on an extensive scale. He may also become involved in quarrels with his people, who may say that he is bad-tempered, while he will say that they are disobedient. Such a dispute will be referred to the mission where an attempt will be made to persuade the two parties to sink their differences. If this fails, the catechist may return to his old village, but may become a catechist elsewhere if the circumstances have not been such as to destroy the mission's confidence in him.

There are other ways in which the catechist represents his village. The post may impose certain responsibilities; thus the catechist may be told to record all live births in the village for the purposes of official statistics. The catechist will try and keep on good terms with the policemen who live at the post and visit the villages. The catechist of Epalanga gave a chicken to a visiting policeman and explained that this was a general practice in order that catechists visiting the post for the annual check on their papers should find a policeman who would be good to them. However, a catechist will object to attempts to associate him with the more unpopular activities of the post. Thus when a policeman came to the Epalanga catechist and asked him to help in recruiting labourers, the latter was rather angry. 'My work is to teach doctrine, not to seize people.' Similarly, when visiting a Protestant village once I asked where the government headman lived and was told in rather an irritated tone, 'No, we have nothing of the post here. We have only the school.'

The sense of responsibility which the catechist feels for his village is sometimes counterbalanced by his lack of effective power. Thus in the dry season of 1956 a bridge near Epalanga which was crossed by the track to Chicunda was broken down. Pedro Chiquete Santos thought that this might bring punishment on the villagers, and accordingly appealed for volunteers to repair it. He also asked Jeremias, the Protestant catechist of

Simbwyikoka, to help. Jeremias turned up with three of his pupils; Pedro, however, had no response. Returning at night to Epalanga, he complained of the attitude of his people, not so much that they had not been ready to help but that they had spread the rumour that he was going to complain to the post. He insisted that he had not said that he would complain to the post; what he had said was that a white labour-recruiter who had had difficulty with the bridge would complain to the post. The attitudes expressed by the catechist are interesting; he feels a responsibility for the village, he has not a corresponding authority to get people to do something which is concerned with the village, but not with the school, but is indignant at the suggestion that he would be willing to denounce his fellow villagers to the post. Indeed, cases arose, which will be described in later chapters, in which a catechist and an elder of the school took an active part in opposing a domineering government headman.

One evening two Kimbundu men, from a different geographical and tribal area, arrived in Epalanga with an unusual story. They had been travelling in the company of a European employer who had suddenly gone off, leaving them without money. This was at a town on the main Luanda–Nova Lisboa road. They had then set out travelling through the villages relying on the hospitality of the catechists to get to the Missão Católica de Bimbe, where they hoped to obtain money to pay bus fares back home. I do not know why they took this way; perhaps as missionary effort to the immediate north of Umbundu country lacks intensity there were no helpful catechists linking the place where they were stranded to their home. What is interesting is that they could rely on the hospitality of the catechists, although they had no kin or tribal bond to appeal to. Here again the catechist appears as the representative of his village who has particular moral duties. Another example of this was when the catechist of Epalanga took part in a funeral as a funeral-friend, which he was, being a native of Ndjandju, the partner-chiefdom of Gumba. He said that he would not take a chicken, as was his right, since he was a catechist, that is, he had special obligations to be generous.

In general the position of the Protestant catechists and elders of the school seems considerably stronger than that of their Catholic counterparts. This impression is gained by visits to Protestant villages and to episodes like that just quoted, where the Protestant catechist had more success than the Catholic in recruiting volunteers for work on the bridge. The reasons for this lie in the organization of the Protestant Church, which owes its origin to Congregationalist missionaries, and in which the distribution of power differs from that in the Catholic Church. The white missionaries exercise only a supervisory role over the work of the Native Church which is responsible for pastoral activity in the villages. The African clergy of the Native Church are entirely dependent financially on their people.

Compared with Catholicism, Protestantism lays much less stress on the sacraments of baptism and communion and much more on Bible-reading and the religious knowledge of the individual. Hence the teaching role of the catechist is more strongly stressed among the Protestants. For example, the Protestant catechists teach girls as well as boys to read and write. His dependence on the clergy is reduced; indeed, owing to the lay participation in the Umbundu Native Church he exercises some control over them. Among the Ovimbundu, as elsewhere in the world, the 'pyramidal' form of Catholicism is absent in Protestantism in which the position of the clergy is weaker and that of the lay leaders strengthened.

The relative autonomy of the Umbundu Native Church vis-à-vis the white missionaries and the disintegration of the traditional system of authority have given judicial powers to its officials. Dr. Childs has written in a recent article:[2] 'In Angola . . . the breakdown of traditional authority has been so rapid that the social life of the villages is now very near to complete anarchy . . . the missions and churches have been compelled to take over. Church leaders—catechists, deacons, and pastors—have taken on judicial functions. Church meetings, both local and regional, have become courts and councils.' He goes on to describe the legalistic attitudes and casuistical morality which is associated with these developments, and suggests that the lack of opportunity for political activity

[2] G. M. Childs, *International Review of Missions*, April 1958.

confines the pursuit of power to the Native Church with un-fortunate results. It might, on the other hand, be suggested that the Protestants among the Ovimbundu are the section of the population who have come nearest to building up new systems of authority and law. It might also be suggested that Umbundu Protestantism retains certain historical features of Congre-gationalism—democratic selection of officials with strict disci-pline binding members of the congregation, industriousness and zeal for education, and a certain consciousness of being a spiritual *élite*.[3]

Another factor in the situation is that the Protestants are a minority compared with the Catholics and tend to have the heightened self-consciousness of religious minorities. They also tend to isolate themselves from the pagans much more than the Catholics do, both geographically by moving into separate hamlets and separate villages and by the greater efforts they make to understand and follow European custom. Protestants for instance seem to know more how the Portuguese kinship terms should be used.

Ultimately, the position of the catechist, whether Catholic or Protestant, is dependent on his role as a teacher of Christian doctrine, and as being a representative of 'modern' values. It may be said that Christian doctrine and 'modern' values are not necessary identical. It is, however, in this field that the Ovimbundu establish their closest contacts with the Europeans. A Protestant explaining why a kinship usage had been dis-continued said: 'We are Christians, we are like the Europeans.' A Catholic catechist arguing the superiority of Catholicism to Protestantism began by saying that the Protestants had no sacraments—then the elder of the school chimed in saying: 'And ours is the religion of the government.' The catechist took up this theme: 'The *chefe de posto* is baptized and married in church, the Governor-General [*sic*] of Nova Lisboa is bap-tized and married in church.' During my first weeks in Epalanga I was asked by the catechist: 'Are there priests in England?' and replied that in England there were both Catholics and Protestants, on which the catechist commented: 'It's the same

[3] For the history of Congregationalism see E. Troelsch, *The Social Teaching of the Christian Churches*, London, 1931, Vol. II, p. 661–6.

thing in Bimbe.' That is, church membership is recognized as giving entry to a world-wide grouping. This sense of being linked to the Europeans by participation in the same sacraments is paralleled on the European side by the custom widespread in Angola of whites standing as godparents to their servants or servants' children. More generally, the missions are regarded as being the cause of that social change which is welcomed by Ovimbundu. Thus the fact that this was 'the time of the school' was given by one of my servants as the reason for such improvements as the decline of sorcery and the increase of cleverness.

Ovimbundu Christians are also aware of the doctrinal significance of baptism—when I asked various people 'Why did you receive baptism?' a general reply would be: 'I want to go to heaven', or some equivalent phrase. The apprehension of Catholic doctrine by the Ovimbundu is a complicated subject. It may be said that the receiving of the sacraments is the aspect of religion that has made most impression on the people. In the conversation previously cited, the catechist began by emphasizing the presence of sacraments as the distinctive mark of Catholicism against Protestantism, and then when the elder of the school pointed to the official associations of Catholicism, the catechist developed this by indicating the receiving of sacraments by those in high office. In the same way a catechist may commend somebody by saying: 'He is baptized and married in Church', as we would say of somebody: 'He is a real Christian'. The contact of the people with the priests, whether at the mission, or in the villages, usually involves the making of confessions and the receiving of communion. Cultural traits particularly characteristic of Portuguese Catholicism are little marked with the exception of the social importance of the godfather-godson tie. Christian ideas of the after-life have penetrated among the pagans, who will say that the soul after death goes to God (Suku) except in the case of bad people who go to hell.

The social relations between Christians and pagans are friendly. The old rites in which the sub-chiefdom as a whole participated have disappeared, and the rites performed at the capital, a liturgy which like other aspects of chieftaincy is a shadow of its former self, arouse little public interest. Christians and pagans co-operate in weddings and funerals. In certain aspects of funeral rites, and in commemorations of ancestors the Christians participate, justifying themselves by arguing that they are purely social functions and have no religious significance. This differs from their attitude to the major exorcism rites,[4] which are avoided by Christians, who regard them with some horror, and towards consulting diviners. Although visiting diviners is strictly forbidden by both Catholic and Protestant missionaries, a high proportion of their people do this,[5] but clandestinely. Thus I was told that there were no diviners in Gumba; in fact, there were two living in Epalanga. It is important to remember that there exist nowadays no pagan 'congregations', that is, permanent groups associated with the performance of ritual.

It is, indeed, through the missions that most of the formal teaching of European culture (apart from the instructions given to labourers and servants) which Ovimbundu receive is given. To the Ovimbundu the missionaries are the Europeans who appear in the most favourable light, and even among pagans the attitude to the missions is without the fear accorded to the post or the suspicion with which the traders are regarded. The missionaries alone run schools, and they provide most of the modern medical services. The missionaries come into far more frequent contact with the people than do the *chefes*, and their relationship with the people is not confined to economics as is that of the traders. The Ovimbundu desire to imitate and learn from Europeans; it is from the missionaries that they have most opportunity of learning, and it is in the African clergy that they have the most clear evidence that this learning from Europeans will bring them results.

The organization of the missions is the form of large-scale social structure with which the people are best acquainted, and with which they are most capable of identifying themselves. A

---

[4] These involve drumming and an open invitation to anybody who wants to turn up. The idea is to persuade the tormenting spirit to pass into a small animal or inanimate object. The minor exorcism (*oku likutilila*) also involves sending the spirit into an inanimate object, but without drumming or the headshaking by the patient which is believed to mark the arrival of the spirit and his acceptance of the offering.

[5] Childs, loc. cit. Personal information.

servant of mine explaining how the Mwekalia chose the chief said, giving me a comparison: 'The Bishop of Nova Lisboa thinks "This priest has sense" and so makes him the superior of a mission'.[6] The disintegration of the old political system, and the association of its representatives with the ritual values which are no longer very significant for the mass of Ovimbundu, has destroyed the old pyramid of authority and prestige. The people associate demands and punishment, for which they seem to receive very little in return, with the post. Many draw a distinction between the actual *chefe* and the government, which they regard as benevolent and ignorant of the behaviour of its representatives. Despite such expressions of loyalty as the singing of the Portuguese national anthem at village parties the 'government' is too distant and shadowy for the Ovimbundu to have much knowledge of it. Nor has the post tried effectively to build up new types of bureaucratic authority in the villages— the government headmen are not given sufficient backing or responsibility by the post to do more than execute its orders.

Hence, the establishment of new types of grouping and leadership at the local level has been the work of the missions, and it is through the missions that these new groupings are articulated on to the total Angolan social system. The missionaries, who provide this articulation between the 'civilized' society and the local organization of the natives, form the section of the 'civilized' population which most satisfies, in its relations with the people, the expectations of the Africans.

To use another term, it is within the Catholic and Protestant Churches that Ovimbundu most clearly identify themselves. Baptism identifies an individual by giving him a name, hence Christians object to non-baptized people identifying themselves in this way. To an individual baptism is significant since it is concerned with his destiny. By it also he identifies himself with the 'civilized' population and achieves a new status superior to that of the pagans. The newly-born child of Christian parents will be given a Christian name and also an Umbundu name from one already held by a dead kinsman.[7] A few villagers

[6] Actually responsibility for appointing superiors of missions largely belongs to the superior of the Nova Lisboa district of the Congregação do Espírito Santo.

[7] For Umbundu names, see Elizabeth Ennis, *African Studies* (Johannesburg) March 1945.

attempt to take on European surnames. Alternatively, a man may take his father's name and attempt to use it as a surname. Thus João Batista Tjindandi, a resident of Epalanga, had received João Batista in baptism, and had taken Tjindandi, his father's name, as a surname. This is, however, not at all a general trend. Even a village of mixed Christian-pagan population may be known by the name of its school, identifying itself by its Christian name.

A man identifies himself also with social change and with progress by 'entering the school'. When a small girl, whom I asked if she had 'entered into the school' replied 'Not at all', her elder sister's husband remarked: 'She is asleep'. In the general Angolan society the religious referent is the most status-giving type of reference that most Ovimbundu can give. There is no very marked feeling in the superiority of one area of Umbundu country to another nor even is there a marked sense of the superiority of Ovimbundu to other tribes—thus the Kimbundu will be highly praised for the degree of European culture they have acquired. The very word Ovimbundu is used as an equivalent of '*pretos*' (blacks) a word not used of 'civilized' Africans, since it is indicative of the lowest colour-class. As a Christian, a man has a status which he shares with Europeans.

He can also identify himself not only in a general way with the Europeans but more particularly with the general church organization. There is much closer contact between the authority-figures of the church organization and the people than between the authority-figures of the administration and the natives. Thus all Catholics in the Nova Lisboa diocese are confirmed by the Bishop of Nova Lisboa, and have seen him— similarly many of the Protestant Ovimbundu know of Dr. Childs, the headmaster of the Protestant secondary school at Dondi, through having heard him preach at a conference. Some Christian villagers would know the names of pioneer missionaries. Little is known by the people about the personalities or duties of the senior members of their administration, and even their titles are not properly understood.

The religious differences which exist at local level have no marked significance in the relations of natives to the post. In certain circumstances a pagan may appeal to a Christian catechist or missionary for support at the post. There is no tendency to confine government appointments to chiefdoms and headmanships to Catholics.[8] However, the Protestant catechists are, unlike the Catholic catechists, not exempt from taxes.[9]

The Ovimbundu no longer possess a coherent political system of their own. They cannot, owing to the nature of their relations with the post and their ignorance of the higher administration, regard the Government as being their representative; the only wide-range systems with which they can identify themselves are the missions. It is through them that the individual is promised eternal life, that the village receives a new type of identity and unity, and that the Ovimbundu as a people participate with the 'civilized' population in ritual communities cutting across the boundaries of culture and geography.

The objection may be made that it is only the Christians who could effectively be represented by the missions and that in Epalanga and Gumba generally baptized Christians formed a minority. It has, however, been previously noted how the school may give its name to a village of mixed population. The catechist will represent both Christians and pagans when he is concerned with the post or with the mission. Moreover, the percentage of pagans in Gumba is far higher than in the rest of Bimbe to which they are linked by the Umbundu language and culture, by administrative divisions, and by a wide range of personal contacts.

It may, then, be asserted, that the catechetical schools and the wider groupings which they build up are the social groups most significant for Umbundu integration on any scale wider than that of the household.

[8] In Gumba the chief and government headman were pagan. There are government-recognized Protestant chiefs elsewhere in Umbundu country.

[9] In some parts of Angola the Catholic catechists are not automatically granted exemption but have to have obtained certain other qualifications, e.g. a certain degree of literacy.

CHAPTER VII

KINSHIP

1. *General Aspects*

A good deal has been said about the contemporary kinship system in Chapter IV, where it was discussed from the point of view of the local organization rather than in its own right. This chapter must, therefore, to some extent, refer to information already presented in Chapters I and IV, since there are three problems to be discussed—the form of the old kinship system, the form of the present kinship system, and the reasons for the changes from one system to the other.

The following approach will be adopted: the ethnographic sources for Umbundu kinship will be examined, information will then be given on the kinship norms formerly valid, and an attempt will then be made to give a coherent sketch of the system then existing. After this, reference will be made to the actual operation of present-day kinship norms and the significance of descent and inheritance. Then factors in the transition between the two systems will be brought forward.

It has been generally accepted by commentators on the ethnographic material that the traditional Umbundu kinship system is of the type called a 'double-descent' system.[1] 'Descent' is used by British anthropologists to imply membership of a group involving rights and duties.[2] Hence, it can only be claimed that the Ovimbundu possessed such a system if there existed two sets of kin groups, and not simply some combination of matrilineal inheritance and virilocal residence at marriage.

One anthropologist, Mr. W. D. Hambly, and two missionaries

[1] For other African double-descent systems see *African Systems of Kinship and Marriage*, ed. Radcliffe-Brown and Forde (Oxford, 1950), pp. 79, 285–359.

[2] The word seems to have been first used in this sense by W. H. R. Rivers.

90

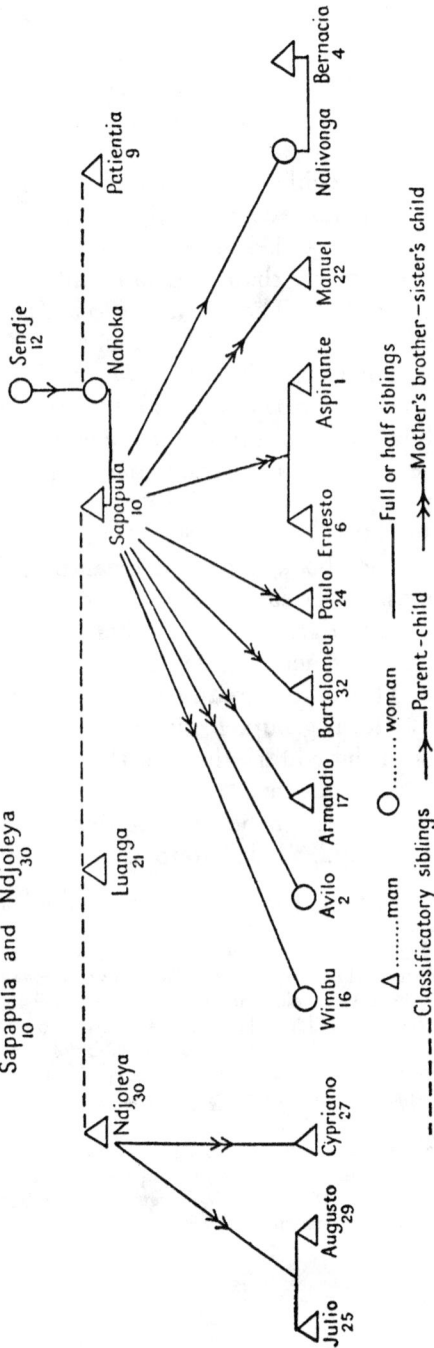

Matrilateral Relationships centred round
Sapapula and Ndjoleya
10   30

Ndjoleya
30

Augusto
29

Julio
25

Cypriano
27

Luanga
21

Sendje
12

Sapapula
10

Nahoka

Patientia
9

Wimbu
16

Avilo
2

Armandio
17

Bartolomeu
32

Paulo
24

Ernesto
6

Aspirante
1

Manuel
22

Nalivonga

Bernacia
4

△ . . . . man   ○ . . . . . . woman

——— Classificatory siblings   ——▶ Parent-child   —————— Full or half siblings

— — — Mother's brother—sister's child

CHART 1. This shows the relationships centred round Sapapula (10) and Ndjoleya (30), the leading personalities of the village. Although they were not directly related there was a link through Luanga (21), who was matrilaterally a 'brother' of Sapapula, and patrilaterally of Ndjoleya. All are living members of the village.

with anthropological knowledge and interests, Dr. Daniel A. Hastings and Dr. Gladwyn Murray Childs, have written on Umbundu kinship.[3] Mr. Hambly's main interest was in material culture and the conditions of his fieldwork were not such as to give him much evidence on the kinship system.[4] Both Dr. Hastings and Dr. Childs recognized the central importance of kinship in Umbundu social life, but have outlined the kinship ties and kinship groups rather than given a detailed analysis.

Mr. Hambly states that 'The phrase *Epata Lia Tate* (or *Oluse*) means "family of my father" and includes all relatives on the father's side. The words *Epata Lia Mai* (or *Oluina*) mean "family of my mother".'[5] This could mean that the Umbundu kinship system is bilateral. He states that inheritance is matrilineal and marriage virilocal, a situation consistent with such a matrilineal kinship system as that of the Bakongo.[6]

Dr. Hastings, whose thesis was completed the year before the publication of Hambly's book, makes it clear that there are two sets of kin groups. 'Over each village is a ruling elder who is the head of the kinship group of that village since all who reside in the village are generally related to him and to each other patrilineally. This elder, greatly revered, is considered the patriarch of that local group. Residence being patrilocal, the office of an elder is hereditary through the male line.'[7] He then goes on to contrast with this, 'the matrilineal sib to which each member is linked, though he may be living in a village away from his sib group.'[8] This group is a clearly defined

[3] Works cited in footnotes to Chapter I. There is a typescript of Hastings's thesis in the library of the International African Institute, London.

[4] Mr. Hambly spent five months in the country, and used as his interpreter and main informant an English-speaking Otjimbundu. He seems simply to have visited villages without living in them. Dr. Childs and Dr. Hastings had both spent several years as 'bush' missionaries. Dr. Childs had actually taken over from Dr. Hastings work in the area to the north-west of Bailundo in the direction of Bimbe, and had subsequently obtained information in Cassongue. He later obtained a good deal of material from African pastors, teachers and schoolboys.

[5] Hambly, pp. 191–2.

[6] For the Bakongo see the discussion by A. I. Richards, in Radcliffe-Brown and Forde, pp. 213–21. Anthropologists have more than once suggested to the author that the Umbundu system was not of the 'double-descent' category but some combination of virilocal marriage and matrilineal descent.

[7] Hastings, p. 16.

[8] Ibid.

social unit. 'All descendants of the same great-great-grand-mother speak of themselves as a group (matrilineally descended), by the term *Imolietu*, i.e. "children from a common source".'[9] Dr. Hastings did not apply the concept of double-descent to this society but regarded it as being matrilineal with patrilineal trimmings. After noting the patrilineal succession to the chiefdom, virilocal residence after marriage, and social preference for patrilineal kinsman, Dr. Hastings states: 'Apart from these apparent indications which might mislead one into concluding that the Ovimbundu are patronymic [*sic*], every other behaviour is obviously linked up as far as social attitudes and relations of the living are concerned within the matrilineal sib.'[10]

The neat tabulation by Dr. Childs[11] of the functions of the two kin groups, when considered in conjunction with the passages cited from Hastings, seems to provide quite clear proof that it is correct to apply the category 'double-descent kinship system' to that formerly prevailing among the Ovimbundu.

2. *Kinship Terms*

Tate	my father	Extended to all brothers, real or classificatory, of a father, all men married to a 'mother', and to the father's sister's son, particularly if he has been your father's heir.
So	your father	
Iso	his father	
Mai	my mother	Extended to all sisters, real or classificatory, of a mother, and to all wives of any 'father'.
Nyoho	your mother	
Ina	his mother	
Sekulu	mother's brother	Extended to any brother, real or classificatory, of a mother, and to the husband of any *apahai*.
Apahai[12]	my father's sister, his father's sister,	Extended to any sister of any father and the wife of any *sekulu*.
Sohai	your father's sister	

[9] Ibid., p. 83. *Imolietu* actually means 'our womb'.

[10] Ibid., p. 87.

[11] Childs, pp. 45–46.

[12] *Tatekai* (father-woman), used in other parts of Umbundu country for 'my father's sister', is not found in Gumba.

The reciprocal of *tate* and *mai* is *omola* (child), usually with the possessive pronoun. *Nungulu* is used for the first-born son, and *kwasula* for the youngest. The reciprocal of both *sekulu* and *apahai* is *otjimumba*. Elder sibling is *huva*, younger sibling is *mandja*, both used with the possessive pronouns. *Kota* seems to have meant formerly the eldest sibling but it is now equivalent to *huva*. *Mukai* is sister, man speaking, and *mume* is brother, woman speaking.

Epalume, pl. *apalume*, cross-cousin
      K'oluse patrilateral cross-cousin
      K'oluina matrilateral cross-cousin

Makulu[13] is used for 'grandfather' and very often for grand-
      mother, though for the latter there is a separate term,
      inakulu; the reciprocal is *onekulu*.

Nawa brother-in-law, sister-in-law. Extended to all siblings, real
      or classificatory, of a wife, the husband of any female
      sibling, and the siblings of such a husband.

Ndatembo father-in-law, mother-in-law;
      son-in-law, daughter-in-law.
      Ndatembo is used only in reference; to address these
      affines one uses *tate* and *mai*.

Tjikwelume[14] sister's daughter's husband, sometimes father's
      sister's husband. The wife's mother's brother may
      be regarded as a mother's brother or as a *ndatembo*.

Tjisoko (funeral friend) is used as a kinship term both in address and reference. This is an abbreviation of the more correct *ukwatjisoko*, of which the plural is *vakwatjisoko*.

The term for wife is *ukai* (woman) or *ufeko* (girl), the latter being perhaps more frequent. *Vey'yange* (my husband) is used as a term of reference by a woman rather than *ulume* (man, husband). Husband and wife would address each other by name or '*a ukuetu*' (O friend). If an individual is both an affine and a kinsman the affinal ties take precedence.

---

[13] Elsewhere *Sekulu* is used for 'grandfather'.
[14] Albino Alves, Vol. I, p. 448, gives *Tjikwelome* as sister's son.

Osanto or *osiala* (namesake) is used as a kinship term, both in address and as reference.

Oluse and *oluina*, which were formerly the words for the agnatic and matrilineal kin group, now mean the patrikin, that is, all to whom one is paternally related, and the matrikin, all to whom one is matrilaterally related. A man, describing a particular tie, may say that it is 'in the matrikin of my father', that is, the relative is a matrilineal kinsman of his father. The terms *onele yohondji* ('the side of the bow') and *onele yohumba* ('the side of the basket') are equivalents of *oluse* and *oluina*.[15] The term *epata* may be used in a general sense for kin but it has very often a primary reference to the matrikin. *Família* (from the Portuguese) means kin in general but it may mean 'kinsman' with reference to a single individual: 'So-and-so is (or is not) my *Família*.' *Ngandi* (which also means 'So-and-so,' equivalent to the Portuguese *fulano*) means kinsman and *usitwe* is kinship.

The use of Portuguese terms is now frequent even among those who do not speak Portuguese. The terms most frequently taken into the Umbundu language are *mano* which is used to mean 'elder brother,' and *mana* which is used to mean 'elder sister,' both terms being used by either sex, *primo* (feminine *prima*), cousin, which is used as an equivalent of *epalume* (cross-cousin), *tio* (uncle), which is now used more frequently than *sekulu*, and *cunhado* (feminine *cunhada*) brother-in-law or sister-in-law, used in the same way as is *nawa*. Ovimbundu villagers talking Portuguese will apply the Portuguese terms in Umbundu style. Thus *irmaõ* (brother) will be used as an equivalent of *mandja* (younger sibling of either sex), and *irmaõ mais velho* (older brother) will be used as an equivalent of *huva* (elder sibling of either sex). Similarly *tia* (aunt) will be used as an equivalent of *apahai*.

The rules about which term may be used in a particular defined relationship (e.g. my wife's mother's brother) are not clearly and exclusively defined. What is more surprising is that a man may not be certain what is the category in which he should class a kinsman with whom he has frequent contacts. Thus Paulo, the elder of the school at Epalanga, often played

---

[15] As noted previously in the references to Chapter I these terms do not seem to have referred to descent groups.

with Adolfo, the small son of Jaime, his wife's brother, but when asked what relation Adolfo was to him, became confused and said, 'My son, my sister's son.'

There exist marked variations in terminology in Umbundu country.[16] For instance, *sekulu* seems to be used for mother's brother only in north-western Umbundu country. Elsewhere *manu*[17] is used for mother's brother, and *sekulu* is used for grandfather. At Caconda, where there has been strong Portuguese influence since the eighteenth century, only the Portuguese kinship terms are known.[18]

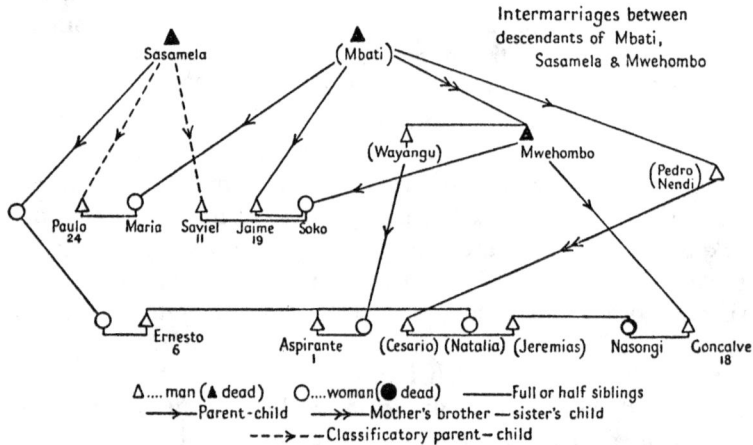

CHART 2. Mbati, Mwehombo and some of their kin. For Mbati (dead, non-member) and Mwehombo (dead, former member) see Chapter III, section 1. For Sasamela (dead, former member) and Cesario, Jeremias, Natalia, Pedro Nendi, and Wayangu (all living non-members) see List II (pp. 55–6). The rest of the individuals named on the chart are members of Epalanga. Paulo and Saviel were 'brothers', both patrilaterally and matrilaterally.

3. Kinship Norms

In this section I shall describe the relations that existed within the elementary family in the time of the rubber trade. A man

[16] For other lists of kinship terms see Hastings, pp. 83–85. Childs, pp. 47–56. M. Howse, *Umbundu Lessons* (Dondi, 1955), Vol. II, pp. 195–7.
[17] Etymologically, *manu* seems to mean 'mother-person'.
[18] Private information.

Sapapula as a
constellation of Kinship ties

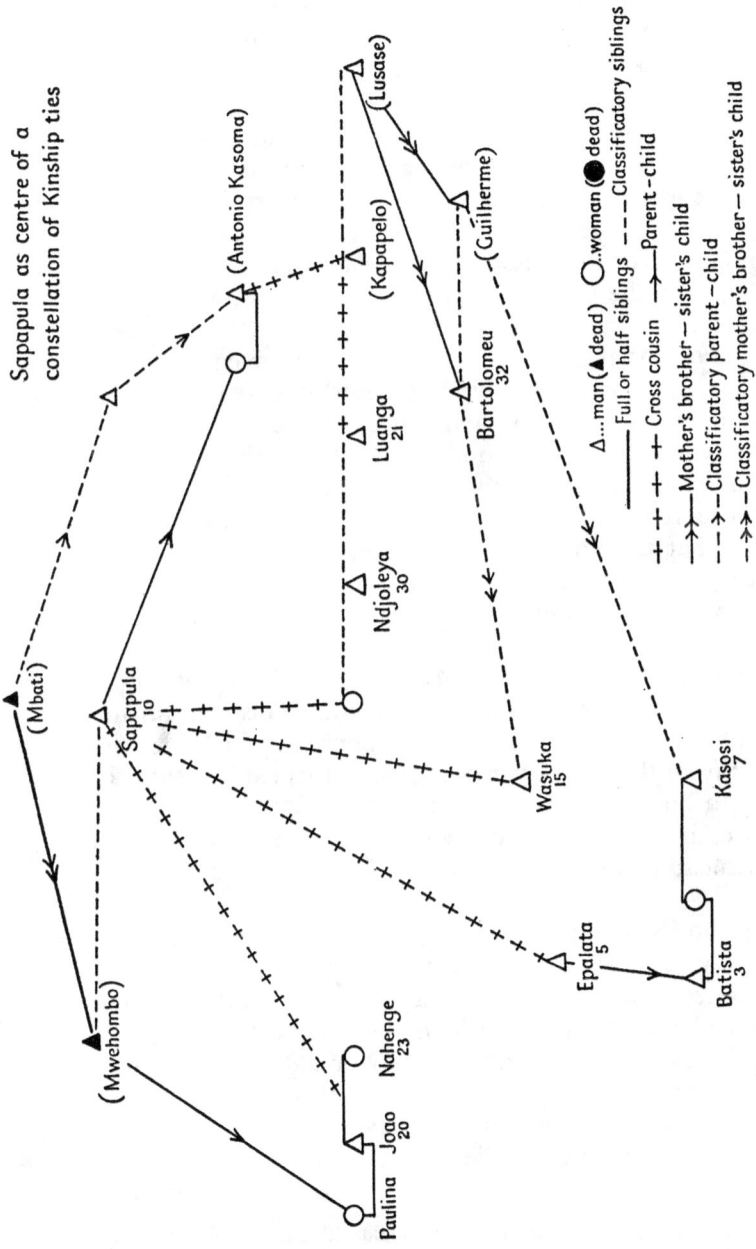

(Mbati)

(Mwehombo)

(Antonio Kasoma)

Sapapula
10

Ndjoleya
30

Luanga
21

(Kappelo)

(Lusase)

Bartolomeu
32

(Guilherme)

Wasuka
15

Kasosi
7

Epalata
5

Batista
3

Paulina

Joao
20

Nahenge
23

△...man(▲dead)   ◯.woman(●dead)   ----Classificatory siblings
———Full or half siblings   ——→Parent-child
+ + +——Cross cousin   ——→
+ + +——Mother's brother — sister's child
——→
- - -→——Classificatory parent -child
+——Classificatory parent -child
- -»→——Classificatory mother's brother — sister's child

CHART 3. Sapapula as the centre of a constellation of kinship ties. It is interesting to note how, in view of the conflict described in Chapter IX, Sapapula is linked to Guilherme, Kapapelo, and Lusase by several paths. All are living members of Epalanga except for Mbati and Mwehombo (for whom see note to Chart 2) and Antonio Kasoma, Guilherme, Kapapelo, and Lusase. For details on these living non-members see List II, pp. 55–6. Not all ties existing between these individuals have been shown.

Correction. The relation of Bartolomeu and Guilherme to Lusase and of Mwehombo to Mbati should be that of classificatory sister's sons.

did not eat or chat with his eldest son or his daughters. Nor did a woman eat or chat with her sons. By 'chatting' I mean a prolonged conversation. It was not forbidden for people in these relationships to speak to one another. Nor could a man eat or joke with his sister (although chatting was permitted) or be alone with her at night. A grown man could not sleep in the same room as his father, except perhaps on a journey, nor could he wear his father's clothes while he was still alive. A grown woman might sleep in the same room as her mother, provided they were far apart.

The reason for these avoidances is usually given simply as 'shame' (osoi) although I have also heard it said in explanation of the father-eldest son avoidance 'If you don't have an eldest son you can't have a family', that is, it is the birth of his eldest son which gives a man status as a father. There seems to be no formalized norm of behaviour towards the *Kwasula*, but it is said that the youngest child is the parent's favourite.[19] When I asked what would happen if a man was alone with his mother at night the answer given was, 'Your father would be angry.'

It is evident that these avoidances would limit the role of the elementary family as an associational unit. This was further limited by the institution of the men's house in which the men and boys from the age of seven or so upwards eat together. In this way, a boy was associated from childhood with the body of agnatic kinsmen from whose conversation he received much of his education in matters ranging from table manners to history.

The authority of a man over his grown sons does not seem to have been very marked. A father had first claim on the services of his adolescent son in the caravan trade; if his father did not need him a lad could travel with another kinsman and a grown man could trade on his own account. Nor did a father apparently control his son's access to land, since this was allocated by the village headman. There was, however, one very important service a father could perform for his son, that of ransoming him when the latter's mother's brother wished to sell him as a

[19] I am not sure if the *kwasula* is the youngest child, either male or female, or the youngest child provided that he is male. I think the latter.

slave. Once ransomed a boy could not be sold again. If, however, the father was displeased with his son's behaviour he could refuse to ransom him. When a man died, his adolescent sons would go to the household of a classificatory father and the children who did not yet 'have sense' would go with the widow to her kin, returning to their agnatic kin when they were older.

4. *Analysis of the Old Kinship System*

The ethnography of the Ovimbundu does show that there existed a double-descent kinship system, each individual belonging to both a local patrilineal group, and a dispersed matrilineal group, in which movable property is inherited. So great has been the impact of social change that not only have these groups disappeared but it is practically impossible to gain additional information on them by direct questions about their nature and functions. The information on kinship norms does give a somewhat clearer picture.

Within the village there was a very strong emphasis on the unity and solidarity of the men of the village. The men's house was the main social centre of the village where the men ate, received guests, and listened to cases. It was about it rather than about the person of the headman that ritual clustered.[20] The elementary family was not the unit of domestic consumption, and it is clear, from the taboos regarding contact with women kin, and the evidence as to the social life of the man's house that there was little recreational contact between the sexes. The concept of *ondjamba*[21] shows that the elementary family of husband, wife, and children, was morally and ritually significant, but many of the educational, nutritive, and recreational functions frequently associated with it were here attached to the men's house.

The strength of the agnatic ties in this society seems to have lain in the solidarity of the men of the village rather than in the patriarchal authority of fathers over sons. A son was economically independent of his father since he could trade on his own while his father was still living; the most powerful social sanction in the hands of kinsmen, that of being sold as a slave, was

---

[20] For these rituals see Hastings, pp. 73–76, and Childs, p. 39.
[21] *Ondjamba* will be discussed more fully in the next chapter.

in the hands of the mother's brother, though the father could, if he wished, intervene; and a man could establish a shrine of his own while his father lived.

It is not altogether easy to see how the matrilineal group maintained its cohesion. It was not the working team on which the caravan trade operated since a man's father had first claim on his services, and he could travel with other relatives. Within it alone loans need not be repaid and accusations of sorcery were made; with this in mind, it is evident why, as Dr. Hastings tells us, people tended to avoid the company of their matrikin, and why most disputes arose in the matrilineal groups.[22] It seems that probably the key to the functioning of the matrilineal groups lies in the details, not now recoverable, of the economy of the caravan trade. As everybody, however successful, was in danger at some time or another of incurring heavy losses,[23] an arrangement by which anybody who was in difficulties could call on his kin for help would be generally acceptable. The association of mutual aid of this sort with matrilineal rather than patrilineal kin would spread losses geographically and would exclude conflicts over currency and movable property from village life. Moreover, the dispersal of the matrilineal kin would provide an individual with business contacts over a considerable area.

5. *Contemporary Kinship Norms*

Much of this has disappeared. The men's house is no longer the dining-room of the village male population. Men now often eat with their wives and children though attitudes and practice of this vary between households. People in their twenties knew of the existence of these avoidance rules but it seems that the rules forbidding sons to eat with their mother and eldest sons and daughters to eat with their father are now generally ignored.

[22] Hastings, pp. 18, 87. Disputes within the matrilineal group could be, and very often were, referred to the sub-chief and king. The account of legal proceedings in Hastings (pp. 139–51) suggests that a high proportion of the cases heard by the kings were to do with sorcery. In such cases the social extension of the matrilineal group beyond the area of the sub-chiefdom and the wider political integration achieved by the kingdoms 'co-operated' in preserving a range of social relations beyond the sub-chiefdom.

[23] Apropos of losses Childs quotes Magyar as saying that the Ovimbundu traded for excitement rather than gain (p. 204).

The rules about avoidance at night are still kept. The prohibitions on a man borrowing his father's clothes and sleeping in the same room as his father seem to survive. The prohibition on a child speaking the name of his father or mother reported by Childs is not, and was not formerly, found in this area. It is, however, wrong for a child to address his parents by name.

Children begin to work in the fields when they are about six. Occasionally boys of 10 to 11 go to the coffee fields for two months work, but usually boys do not go out to work until they are about 14 or 15.

A boy going out to work should ask his father's permission to go though this is not always done. Returning from work whether contract labour or voluntary work a boy should bring presents to his relatives. He would be expected to give something, say, a jacket, to his father, and a cloth to his mother, on returning from voluntary work and a shirt to his father on coming back from contract labour. These gifts should be made in kind. Money lent from son to father should be repaid, though it is wrong for a son to enforce payment by appealing to the post for policemen. A father may give money to his son for bride-wealth, and may suggest a choice of bride. He cannot constrain, nor could he in the past, his son and daughter to a marriage they do not wish.

A man cannot be said to have real authority over his grown sons. The stated norm is that a man's sons stay in the same village till he dies. He has no power to make them do so, and they are not condemned by public opinion if they live elsewhere. A man's attitude to classificatory 'fathers' is determined by the age, status, and personalities of those involved, rather than by jural rights and obligations. I have found men unable to tell me what had become of their own brothers' children.

Formerly when the father of an adolescent boy died he would join the household of a father's brother. Nowadays this would be much less likely, as it is common for such a boy to settle with other categories of kin, notably siblings and maternal kinsfolk. A man is free to stay with his brothers if he wishes, or to leave them.

While the tie between full brothers is held to be the strongest, as regards classificatory brothers there seems to be a slight leaning towards matrilateral rather than patrilateral brothers. The classificatory kinship terminology, and the lack of genealogies and kinship groups, means that a man knows a great many classificatory brothers living in his neighbourhood of whom he vaguely recognizes some as 'close' others as 'distant', but with whom his relations are not especially significant. A boy or girl who loses his or her parents is fairly likely, judging from the evidence of Epalanga households, to settle with a full- or half-brother or sister.

Formerly, owing to virilocal marriage, a sister was geographically separated from her brother, and even if widowed or divorced would not necessarily return to his village, but might go to her mother's brother.[24] With this geographical separation went a situation of possible conflict, since the brother could sell his sister's children to recoup his own debts, and the shadow of sorcery fears seems to have touched this relationship.[25] The suppression of the rubber and slave trades and the subsequent disintegration of the kinship groups have removed the economic pressures which made for conflict between matrilineal kin and the residence rules which divided people locally into groups of agnates and their wives. The brother-sister tie has therefore changed its content, since it is released from the heavy pressures formerly active in the matrilineal kin groups.

It would be wrong to produce any such generalization as 'a woman must always be under the guardianship of a male relative'. A woman who is widowed or divorced or whose husband is away working will tend, however, to develop a particular link with the male head of some household, her own kinsman usually, except in the case of a labour migrant's wife, when it may be a kinsman of her husband. Thus in Epalanga, Augusto (25) aided the household of his absent full brother Julio (29).

Aid is most likely to be given to a kinsman's wife when the two households are close together. The underlying idea seems to be to keep the kinsman's household together rather than any duty of aiding an affine. For a widow or divorced woman or the

---

[24] Childs, pp. 25–37.

[25] H. W. Nevinson (*A Modern Slavery*) gives a complicated story which suggests this possibility (p. 101).

wife of a 'lost' labour migrant the tie with the brother or other kinsman will be more important, though the degree to which there is contact between the two households will vary.

It would seem that the present significance of the brother-sister tie is due to the frequency and likelihood of husbands being away from villages as labourers. The strength of this tie gives added significance to the mother's brother—sister's son tie.

A sister's son traditionally inherited his mother's brother's movable property, and during his lifetime might borrow from him without need of repayment. Against this, the mother's brother had the right to sell his sister's son as a slave and it was he who was considered most likely, both traditionally and at the present day, to practise sorcery against his sister's son. My informants were divided as to whether the sister's son can practise sorcery against his mother's brother. However, it was stated by Hastings[26] and by my informants that sorcery was only practised between matrilineal kin. It is not easy to see how in the past the relationship between a man and his mother's brothers operated—to what extent a man had particular expectations and obligations to one particular mother's brother rather than to the whole set of senior matrilineal kin.

At the present time the content of the relationship between mother's brother and sister's son seems very fluid, depending on age and personal compatibility. An important difference arises between one's attitude to 'mother's brothers' and to 'fathers'. There is no strong tie with one's mother's own brother, as there is with one's own father; on the other hand, a boy whose father has died is regarded as much more likely to go to the house of a classificatory mother's brother than to the house of a classificatory father, although, as has been noted, children and adolescents may settle with kin of other categories.

Traditionally the relationship between a man and his wife's brother was distant and reserved, the two men being forbidden to eat together or joke. Nowadays the relations between a man and his wife's full or half brother are often very friendly; quite often when one finds two households close together they turn out to belong to men related in this way.

A brother-in-law is not regarded as a kinsman—he does not

[26] Hastings, p. 87.

have a kinsman's obligation to lend money in case of need if he has it, and it is said that one should only work very occasionally with a brother-in-law. When I asked which a woman preferred, her husband or her brother, men told me that she liked both equally, and the fact that a man and his wife's brother often live close together confirms that there is relatively little for them to quarrel over. A woman does not establish close ties with any of her affines. Formerly, when a man died leaving a widow (and according to some informants a small child) a patrilateral cross-cousin of his might marry her. My informants, however, denied that a sororate had existed even in the past.[27]

Cross-cousins are the relatives with whom solidarity is most strongly felt. When I asked about the relationship between full siblings I was told 'They like each other just as cross-cousins do.' Now that it is no longer customary for agnatic kin to live together, it is often said that it is good to live near cross-cousins.

Formerly funeral friendship (*ukwatjisoko*) was part of an alliance between sub-chiefdoms, which were not contiguous. Nowadays, since people move about the country, funeral friendships may be regarded as another category of kinship— when one asks a man his relationship with somebody else this may be given. There is a tendency to regard *vakwatjisoko*, funeral friends, as being a sort of cross-cousins since both perform funeral services. This survival of funeral friendship, as a tie between individuals and as a haphazard means of supplying undertakers, exists in Gumba. In Ndjandju, which is the sub-chiefdom in which the Missão Católica de Bimbe is built, the *tjisoko* relationship is now established between two neighbouring villages and is apparently the normal means of performing burials, and the permitted theft of small livestock regularly takes place.

Between parents-in-law and children-in-law the relation was and is one of restraint. This is most marked in the relations between in-laws of opposite sex, and least between the mother-in-law and daughter-in-law.

[27] See Albino Alves under (*o*)*mingandjo*, for evidence of a sororate in some Umbundu areas.

6. *Descent, Inheritance and Succession*

There is little interest in genealogical detail among contemporary Ovimbundu, which is not surprising since there exists no system of descent groups in which the position of the individual may be genealogically defined nor does affiliation to a particular line of descent give status *vis-à-vis* people of less eminent descent. Pedigrees are traced (in either line) for only two to four ascending generations though one man I met could name ancestors for nine ascending generations.

Despite this vagueness and lack of interest in the articulation of relationships, Ovimbundu will say that such-and-such a kinsman is 'close' and such-and-such is 'distant' even though they cannot fit this into a genealogical framework. 'Closeness' and 'nearness' are not simply used to refer to geographical proximity or social co-operation, since there may be much mutual assistance between kinsmen who are 'distant'. One might speak of a blurred edge of kinship not clearly defined in categories of kin but not non-kinsmen. A man may speak of somebody on this 'blurred edge' thus: 'He must be a kinsman but I don't know how.' Similarly the *vakwatjisoko* are a class of people who are not definitely kin, and not non-kin.

There is little formalized distinction between patrikin and matrikin. There is a certain matrilateral pull in the choice of residence, a man being, as has been noted, more likely to settle with a mother's brother than with a 'father'. I had the impression that a man is more likely to settle with a matrilateral 'brother' than with a patrilateral one, but it would be very difficult to establish this by quantitative methods owing to the complexity of the factors affecting residence. As a man tends to settle where he has a number of kin rather than in the shelter of one particular kinsman, this trend does not lead to the formation of matrilineal clusters of kin. The majority of informants still consider that sorcery can only be practised among matrilineal kin but for various reasons it may be said that the fear of sorcery is not significant in kinship relations.[28]

[28] It may be suggested that the disappearance of the matrilineal groups which imposed a co-operation involving exacting demands has been paralleled by the decline of sorcery, the mystical reflection of underlying tensions. How is the fact that several informants told me that sorcery had declined since the days of the

Inheritance of movable goods was traditionally entirely matrilineal. Today informants are confused as to what ought to be done. Inquiry about particular cases will reveal that often no movable property was left by the deceased, it having been used to pay for such expenses of the illness and funeral as the purchase of medicines and the buying of animals to be slaughtered at the feasts.

Where there is movable property, the transmission of it to the heirs is carried out in a rather informalized way, as so often happens in Umbundu social activities. The actual division of property is undertaken by a kinsman of the deceased. This should apparently be the most senior kinsman. It may be a cross-cousin or 'brother' or a sister's son.[29] How it is decided who is the senior kinsman, and who are fitted to participate in the share-out is not very clear. Nor does it seem that there is any effective device against the sharer-out giving himself the lion's share, except the general pressures and reciprocities of kinship. The principle accepted in the share-out is that inheritance should be a reflection of the relations which existed with the dead man, and also be a reward of funeral services. Nothing is kept for kin who are away working, and a son who did not keep in contact with his father would be omitted from the share-out.

By inheritance a man can increase his small stock of possessions. He is unlikely to receive anything much in the way of money, and since there is no land shortage, and, as yet, little in the way of valuable immovable property such as brick

---

rubber trade to be reconciled with the statement by Childs that fear of sorcery was increasing (Childs pp. 57–58)? I suggest that the final disintegration of the old kinship groups may have been marked by particularly sharp social tensions, but that once these groups were in fact dissolved and a new form of social relations established the fear of sorcery may have declined. It should also be remembered that as indicated in Chapter V the present-day economic values of the Ovimbundu do not lead to expectations that a prosperous individual will share his wealth with poorer kinsmen, as was the case in the time of the rubber trade. Hence accusations of sorcery based on disappointed expectations of generosity are unlikely to arise.

Another aspect of the question which cannot be explored here in detail is the lack of agreement on the causality of classes of happenings or individual events. Thus one informant will say that a woman's pains in childbirth are due to sorcerers among her kin, another will say that they are caused by God (as we would say, are natural).

[29] Hambly, pp. 199–200.

houses, coffee plants and so on there is little likelihood of disputes arising about the inheritance of land claims. A woman's
property should be given to her sisters, after her children have
had their cut. In one case a man inherited his sister's debts but
allowed her children to inherit her property, 'lest they be sad'.
A wife's fields return to her husband.

Inheritance is then a process by which the relations of certain
kin, both sons and sister's sons, with the deceased are recognized
by the transmission of his property. As with other aspects of
Umbundu kinship, while the existence of the kinship tie provides the basis on which to found a relationship, its content is
determined by the nature of the contacts between the individuals involved and the services given.

Although there is a definite tendency for men of chiefly stock
to have longer pedigrees than other individuals there is no
chiefly genealogy. When Paulo, the elder of the school of
Epalanga, told me that had he not been blind he might have
been chief of Gumba, he quoted the names of four chiefs to
whom he was related. The chieftancy is not tied to a lineage,
but can be held by any individual who can claim links with a
former chief or chiefs. People 'of the blood of the chiefs' in no
sense form a differentiated group of aristocrats significant in
social life.

In similar fashion membership of the spirit-linked professions and of certain cults seems to have been a matter of succession of one individual to the role of another.[30] Membership
of the hunting and smithing professions descended patrilineally,
but if a hunter or smith had no son his position could be succeeded to by a daughter's son.[31]

7. *Kinship in a Changing Society*

From this, and from other chapters, a picture of Umbundu
kinship may emerge as something so blurred, confused, and
confusing, as hardly to merit the term 'kinship system', yet at

[30] i.e. rather than admission to a corporate group of hunters. A man can inherit
his father's hunting spirit before the latter's death; in Epalanga Batista had
received the hunting spirit of his father Epalata.

[31] My informants were not agreed as to whether a sister's son could inherit in
default of a son.

the same time clearly an important part of social life. Kinship norms are confused, as is the correct term to use in a particular relationship. Ritual and jural sanctions are lacking, as are institutions based on the regular co-operation of groups of kinsmen. Yet a man likes to live with kinsfolk and there is a tendency for kin to cluster together in a neighbourhood.

By the very facts, that so many of a man's neighbours are his kinsmen, and that there is very little marked differentiation between the behaviour towards different categories of kin, kinship is robbed of any great specificity of content. It might be said that it is the quantity rather than the quality of kinship ties that makes kinship significant in establishing a 'sense of community' in a neighbourhood, in that the multiplicity of local kin ties creates some identification between a man's range of kin and his neighbourhood. At the same time a kinship tie provides a basis on which a closer relationship may be built by reciprocal services. It appears that the inheritance of property recognizes kinship in this way by recognizing claims not on the basis of strict genealogical proximity but on the quality of the relationship.

A discussion of marriage and the household must be left to the next chapter. The outline given of the present kinship system is sufficiently clear to begin an examination of the reasons for the changes. This must rely to some extent on speculation, owing to a lack of information on the actual working of the kinship system while it was in transition to its present form.

The key change is the disappearance of the kinship groups. These, it seems, disappeared because of their high degree of dependence on the particular type of economy existing before 1911. It has already been argued that the distinction between the patrikin and the matrikin is an attempt to isolate economic claims and conflicts from village and political relationships, and that the giving of loans without right of repayment within the matrikin was called for by a trading system in which credit played an important part. With the end of the trade the wealth passing through Umbundu hands declined sharply, and there was neither need for funds to meet trading losses nor currency to provide them. A man obtained money either by growing crops helped by his wife and children or by going out to work. Neither means of making money involves regular co-operation with a body of kinsmen. The occasional co-operation needed in situations of financial crisis or mutual help for some particular job can be provided by those of a man's numerous kinsfolk with whom he has established ties of amity above the mere recognition of relationship.[32]

The disappearance of the matrilineal group was a logical consequence of the disappearance of its *raison d'être*. With the disappearance of the matrilineal group, there was no longer any need to preserve the distinctive nature of the agnatic group. It is quite possible to suppose that the village might have preserved its patrilineal base if other factors had come into play. Such possible factors would be a shortage of land, danger of attack from enemies, or the use by the headman of his political power to keep control over his patrikin.[33]

A question of some significance arises from the differences of attitude to a man's 'fathers' and to his 'mother's brothers' which has been noted earlier on. From the literature it might seem that the link between agnates was very strong, and that it is surprising that it should have broken up so completely. It may be suggested that the unity of agnatic kin was expressed in the idiom of relations between villagers rather than of relations between kin, and that within the village there was not necessarily much greater solidarity between siblings than between distant agnates. The solidarity of paternal siblings was then, granting this hypothesis, a reflection of the wider solidarity of the village. When the village disintegrated the close ties between brothers disintegrated also.

The unity of the matrikin was perhaps expressed to a much greater degree in a kinship idiom.[34] This is perhaps one of the

[32] The amount of aid an·individual can mobilize in case of need depends to a very great extent on personal factors. It should be emphasized that it is personal co-operation over a number of years rather than any genealogical nearness that inclines a man to be helpful. While helpfulness to kinsfolk is a norm of Umbundu ethics, it is possible in practice to provide excuses for non-co-operation.

[33] The rapid disintegration of the indigenous system of authority after the middle thirties may reasonably be linked with the decay of agnatic ties of residence.

[34] 'When an Ocimbundu speaks of his family (*epata*) in the sense of a large and widespread organization with a recognized head in some elder, it is generally his *oluina* to which he refers.' Childs, p. 44.

reasons behind the 'neo-matrilineal' pull in residence, the other being the new relationship between brother and sister, with its consequent influence on the mother's brother—sister's son relationship.

In this chapter on the kinship system the preferential marriages have not been discussed at length, but without them the contemporary kinship system would not tie up as it does with the local organization. The next chapter complements this one.

CHAPTER VIII

MARRIAGE

━━━∿∿∿∿∿∿∿/⊙/∿∿∿∿∿━━━

1. *The Significance of Preferential Marriage*

Informants say that it is permissible to marry a classificatory cross-cousin, are divided as to the permissibility of marriage with a classificatory sister's daughter, and generally disapprove of marriage with other kin categories, or with true kin of these two categories. Indeed, kinsfolk who marry seem usually not to have any traceable common ancestor.[1] Up to recently,[2] a man marrying a kinswoman had to pay an indemnification of, say, 20 escudos to 'cut the blood'. This changed the kin relationship into an affinal one.

It has been previously stated that preferential marriages have an important social role to play in keeping kinsfolk together and multiplying the ties of kinship and affinity. If this is to be proved, it is necessary to show what the people themselves think of preferential marriages, what proportion of the marriages are between kinsfolk, whether this proportion has decreased under modern conditions, and how it relates to the contemporary kinship system.

Several reasons may be given for choosing a cross-cousin bride. The bridewealth is likely to be lower, the girl is more likely to stay and not run away, if one cannot find another girl there will always be a cross-cousin to marry, and, old men point out, one will not be fined if a cross-cousin bride dies.

---

[1] This statement does not depend simply on my own information. Padre Feltin, superior of the Bimbe mission, who knew of the existence of these marriages told me that very few Umbundu marriages were between kin within the degrees of kinship prohibited (a prohibition removable by a dispensation) by the Catholic Church. Marriage with a first cousin is not infrequent both in Portugal itself and among the white Portuguese in Angola.

[2] About 1949.

Another explanation, which I have quoted earlier, is that if one marries a kinswoman, one's children, when they grow up, will not leave, since they see 'a cross-cousin here, a cross-cousin there'.

All these reasons are no doubt to some extent valid. There are no fixed limits for bridewealth and no doubt some bride-wealths paid in a cross-cousin marriage are higher than some paid in marriages between non-kin; however, it is generally held that a kinsman is less demanding over the question of bridewealth than a non-kinsman. There is some evidence that cross-cousin marriages are more stable than those with non-kinsfolk. The high proportion of cross-cousin marriages naturally leads to an individual tending, when considering the possibility of marriage, to think of his female kin, even though there is no individual girl whom he is expected to marry.

The custom of fining a man whose wife had died was noted among the Ovimbundu a hundred years ago by Ladislau Magyar; in recent times it seems to have disappeared from most of Umbundu country. Its survival in Gumba up to the last few years may be related to the links existing between Gumba and the northern non-Umbundu peoples, who apparently practise it to this day.

The last of the explanations given may be translated thus, 'Cross-cousin marriage means that the children will have the same individuals as both patrikin and matrikin. They will remain in their father's village, where he is living with his kin and will not be inclined to return to their matrikin.' This line of argument comes close to the 'observer' explanation previously offered that preferential marriage greatly increases the number of social relations within a neighbourhood. The Ovimbundu do not see this aspect of cross-cousin marriage, and this fits their lack of any 'model' of their own society as a whole, which is in turn a consequence of the rapid social change they have experienced. However, they do see cross-cousin marriage as increasing the number of ties which exist for an individual in his village and neighbourhood.

The diagrams and information contained in Chapter IV have already indicated how individuals are linked by marriage ties, and in Chapter VII the way in which brothers-in-law may live next to each other has been noted as a new development, impossible in the days of agnatic residence groups. It will be remembered how in listing the kinship cores of Epalanga, Joaõ was placed among the kin of Mbati and Mwehombo with which he had become associated through his marriage to Paulina, although he had come to Epalanga through his relationship to Sapapula.

I have earlier described the preferential marriages as giving 'stability' to the kinship system and as providing a limit on the spread of affinal ties. In what does this stability consist, and how far is there really a limit?

The stability given by the marriage system is not the sum of the stability of individual marriages. Nor is it more than partially a local stability; marriages are not limited to a small geographical range, although the network of marriages between kin is very significant in local relations and even 'long distance' marriages which renew links with Cela and Namba reflect long-standing contacts of marriage and migration. The stability lies in the 'pattern' by which new preferential marriages are constantly being made.

The socio-geographical range over which wives are found does not differ appreciably from the socio-geographical range over which kin ties exist, which, as has been noted in Chapter IV[3], links Gumba strongly to Cassongue, Cela, and Namba, rather than with areas to the south and east, and this range does not seem to be expanding under modern conditions. Migrant labourers do not return to Gumba with wives from other areas. The only definite exception I knew to this rule was provided by Sawaisi, a traditional village headman, who had travelled on the caravans and had subsequently been a soldier. Stationed at Luanda he had there married three Kimbundu women with whom he returned to Gumba, where they were still living with him during my stay.

The preference for kinship marriage is not a limiting factor on marriage in the way that a rule of endogamy is, since a number of marriages occur with non-kinswomen. It is a limiting factor in the way that it gives an additional significance to kinship, since in the choice of a wife the distinction between kin and

[3] See p. 58.

non-kin, which is not marked in ordinary social life, becomes important. Kinship marriages transform 'distant' kin ties into close affinal ties which will in the next generation become close kinship ties.

It is extremely difficult even to guess how this system operated in the past. Did the high rate of preferential marriages have the same function formerly as now? Or has the institution continued in being, while its function relative to the total society has changed? The testimony of that informant of Dr. Childs who told him that formerly all marriages were kin marriages and that patrilaterally one only married on 'the side of the basket' and matrilaterally only on 'the side of the bow'[4] has led Professor Barnes to suggest[5] that the preferential marriages functioned as links between descent groups. Both Dr. Childs and myself, however, have found that 'the side of the bow' and 'the side of the basket' are simply synonyms for 'oluse' and 'oluina'.[6] Moreover, my informants did not confirm his statement since they denied the right of marriage with a father's sister, and the quantitative information shows that even in the past some marriages were with non-kinswomen, and that others were with categories of kin theoretically forbidden, so that, then as now, the preferential marriages were with distant kinswomen rather than with a specific category of kin.

If, however, kinship marriages in the past operated as they now do, it is difficult to see their relation to the patrilineal and matrilineal groups. A clue to a solution is surely given by the custom of 'cutting the blood', which destroyed kinship to begin affinity. Marriages were arranged, it may be suggested, with those people who were still just kin, and who probably often were also geographically as well as socially distant so that the number of ties outside the sub-chiefdom might be increased, a matter of importance for long-distance traders. Later, Portuguese rule made travel no longer dependent on such long range contacts. Meanwhile the disintegration of the agnatic residence

---

[4] The exact words are 'Formerly people never married unless they were related, that is to say unless they touched the blood together. If in the mother's kin (k'oluina) only on the side of the bow (i.e. male line). If in the father's kin (k'oluse) only on the side of the basket (i.e. female line)'. See Childs, pp. 53–56.

[5] Review of Childs in *Man*, 1950, pp. 126–8.

[6] Dr. Childs was speaking to me apropos of Barnes's interpretation.

groups began to make the socio-geographical function of these marriages no longer the renewal of ties with distant kin but the holding together of the local community no longer held in the firm framework of the old local organization.

Several explanations can therefore be given for preferential marriages. From the point of view of the man making such a marriage there are economic advantages in the probably lower bridewealth and, formerly, the avoidance of the fine payable on the death of a non-related wife. The marriage itself is more likely to be stable, and a man's children are more likely to stay with him if they have other kin close at hand. The local mobility of the Ovimbundu to some extent assists marital stability, since a bride arriving in a village may well find there other kin than her husband and his relatives, and may find such relatives helpful to her.

From an observer's view-point, preferential marriage is important on the village and neighbourhood level by multiplying social links within them. Its importance for the kinship system lies in its giving significance to the distinction between kin and non-kin and in keeping kinsfolk together without either localization of kinship groups or villages with strong headmen.

2. Husband, Wife, and Household

Traditionally the Ovimbundu lived chastely till marriage, and there existed sanctions in the form of fines, alterations in the marriage ceremony, and mystically caused illness, against unchastity.[7] The force of these sanctions has weakened in modern times;[8] however, many Ovimbundu remain chaste until marriage.

The age of marriage is about twenty-two for a man, and about eighteen for a girl. In Gumba there is some tendency to marry younger at about 16–17. Villagers in Epalanga ascribed this to contract labour, that is, to the necessity of a contract labourer having to have someone to cook for him. This is a point which will be considered later in reference to the wife's services to her

[7] Hastings, p. 121. Childs, p. 113.

[8] Childs, loc. cit., and fieldwork.

husband. Another explanation is that this is a northern practice which has spread into Gumba.[9]

A young man who wishes to marry approaches the girl of his choice and asks her to marry him. He then asks her parents for their permission. The consent of both partners and of their parents is required now as in the past, though parental consent may often be evaded by running off to the towns and getting married there. After that negotiations are conducted with a senior kinsman as intermediary. Before the marriage can take place, bridewealth must be paid over. It is this that gives the right to claim damages for adultery. When asked why bridewealth is paid, informants are likely to say that it compensates the father for the expense of the bringing up of his daughter.

The amount of bridewealth paid has been rising. Two informants said that four yards (metres) of cloth and a bottle of rum formed the bridewealth in the time of the rubber trade. Others suggested as the bridewealth of that period a hoe and a few sleeping-mats. Alternatively seashells or even Portuguese coins, which were not then used in transactions among the Ovimbundu, were employed. These bridewealth objects were obtained from outside Umbundu country and had a certain rarity value, unlike the other objects which were very common. In the early thirties Hastings also mentioned the bridewealth as consisting of four yards of cloth, a bottle of rum, plus a kerchief given to her father's sister.[10] Money seems to have come in as a regular part of bridewealth about 1940.

When Cypriano married in 1949 Rosa, a sister's daughter, he paid 200 escudos (about £2. 10s.), a black cloth to her mother, and a small pig to her father. When Pedro Epalanga Chimbalanya married, near the Bimbe mission, in 1955 he paid 400 escudos, one cloth of six metres, a head cloth, a woman's blouse, and a bottle of rum. When in 1956 Daniel married Feliciana, a sister's daughter of Ndjoleya and his cross-cousin, he paid 400 escudos, whereas when Jose the son of Paulo married in the same year he paid 300 escudos also for a cross-cousin.

The bridewealth should be paid to the father. If however, a

---

[9] Explanation given by Padre Feltin.
[10] Hastings, p. 95.

for the bride's village. Here they may be greeted with formal speeches of welcome in Portuguese, a usage copied from the reception of missionaries.

One only turns up to a wedding if one has been invited, and not everybody who is a kinsman living in the neighbourhood is invited. Nor is there any marked distinction between kin and non-kin in the ceremony, except for the ending of avoidances and the recognition of the father's sister, who is recompensed for her services as nursemaid. Village membership is significantly recognized in the distribution of food, and the sending of the party to the bride's home to represent the bridegroom's village.

Umbundu marriage is virilocal, although a certain number of marriages are within the village. Apart from such marriages, it seems to be rare to find a man settling in a village because his wife has kin there.

Although during the early months of the marriage the bridegroom's mother may supervise the bride's work, the individual household is essentially an independent unit[13] and was not even in the past merged with other household units to form a 'grandfamily'. This independence is not isolation. I have only a very few times seen houses with any sort of compound about them. Much of domestic life, eating, working, resting, talking, may be done out of doors in front of the house. Paying visits is a great feature of village life especially when the day's work is over, although there is also a term *oku pasula*, to visit in the morning, referring to what are usually just short calls, involving the exchange of greetings. Perhaps the opportunity of calling and being called on is one of the factors maintaining the village as a social unit. The idea that a man should not eat with his wife still survives to some extent so that questions on this topic receive contradictory answers. Observation shows that even among the men who travelled on the caravans, eating with one's wife is the general practice.

One of the most striking features of Umbundu domestic life is the close companionship which exists between husband and wife and which is unquestionably a modern development.[14]

[13] See Magyar, pp. 281–3.
[14] The role of the *Ondjango* as described by Childs and Hastings indicates that a man's normal companions both for eating and recreation were other men.

Going round the houses at night one meets in one house a man and his wife sitting together talking, in another a group of men and women sitting round a fire. This is a very definite change from traditional pattern of social life in which men and women sat in separate groups, a pattern which is still observed at funerals.[15] A man who has a case at the post is likely to take with him his wife as a witness. A husband has the right to beat his wife, and she should show respect to him. In fact wife-beating is rare, and the relationship seems from observation to be often one of mutual affection and close companionship. Informants were divided as to whether one can joke with one's wife—some people may fear that she will cease to respect her husband if he jokes with her—but conversationally an Umbundu wife often seems to enjoy an easy familiarity with her husband. A wife may occasionally go and stay with her relatives, and in the neighbourhood she may pay calls on kinsfolk, friends, or co-villagers, without her husband. This contrasts with the way the white and mulatto wives of traders follow the custom of rural Portugal by staying more or less permanently in the house.

The wife has her own fields, and her own granary. If the marriage is polygamous, each wife has her field and granary. Her husband may help her in her fields, although he also has fields of his own. The maize in the husband's granary is sold to produce money to pay tax and to buy clothing for both husband and wife, and the maize in the wife's granary is used for food. If her husband is away a woman will buy her clothes from her own granary. The cooking of maize has not only a nutritive importance but also a social one since it is considered the service, which is specifically wifely. Thus, the explanation I was given for the lower age of marriage emphasizes this—I should explain that people returning from contract labour are sent first to the post at which they were recruited and may have to do an additional fortnight's work there. 'It is because of the hardship.[16] In the past one married only when one was fully grown. Now it is necessary to have somebody who will send food to the post when you come back.' 'Perhaps,' I suggested, 'your mother

[15] Childs, pp. 32, 35.
[16] *Ohali*, a word often used with regard to administrative demands.

could send food.' 'Perhaps your mother is dead, and she has to think of your father.' A man should not cook for himself in a village, by a rule of convention which has no sanction attached, although he may do so when away working.

Clearing fields, house-building, and thatching are men's work, as are brick-making, fishing, hunting, mat-making, sewing, and woodwork. Beer-brewing, cooking, maize-pounding, and water and firewood gathering are women's work. Men and women can work together in most forms of agriculture, sowing, hoeing, harvesting, feeding small stock and treating tobacco. The division of labour is based on ideas of what is natural and fitting, not on any sanctions, mystical or otherwise. Nor is the division always strictly observed. A man may fetch water if his wife is ill, or simply away visiting relatives, and I have seen an adolescent boy pounding out maize on a pounding-block.

A man should look after his sick wife. There is a song which is sung about the married couples of the village, each being named in turn, which tells how the husband went to the post and his wife climbed a tree to get some fruit down. She fell down and hurt herself and then wailed because there was nobody to look after her. A woman who is ill for some time will return to her kin to get better.

The husband does not attend his wife's funeral, but washes himself all over, and then has to lie down asleep, or as if sleeping, during the funeral. Grains of maize and other crops may be, but are not always, even at pagan funerals, thrown over a woman's coffin as it is taken to the cemetery. A man should leave his old home when his wife dies, although this rule is neglected nowadays, certainly by the owners of brick houses. After a year or two, a widower should *oku wonga*, pile up stones on his wife's grave, a duty which has behind it a vague mystical sanction of illness. The widow of a hunter should be buried beside her husband even though after his death she has married again.[17]

A widow may marry again about six months after the funeral. The exception to this is the *inakulu*, the chief's main wife. Formerly, it was permitted for a widow to marry her husband's

[17] A case of this occurred during my stay.

patrilateral cross-cousin, the reason for this being apparently to enable him to look after the children. Other marriages of a widow with her dead husband's kin were and are forbidden under pain of mystical sanctions. Thus, marriage with one's dead wife's sister would lead to the latter's death through her sister's spirit. Illness or death was suggested as the penalty for marriage with a mother's brother's widow, although I know of two cases of such marriages happening. The reason for this prohibition against any marriage by a widow or widower with the kin of a deceased spouse is given as being that it is wrong to mix the blood.

Adultery is subject to mystical sanctions in the illness called *ondjamba* which seems to involve swelling of the legs. This afflicts not the guilty party but the other spouse (whether husband or wife) and the children.[18] I was also told by some informants that this illness affected the other spouse if there were no children; if there were children adultery would endanger their lives and the life of the innocent spouse. Some people do not believe in this nowadays; however the line between believers and non-believers cannot be equalled with that between pagan and Christian or old and young. It is of course impossible to say how frequent adultery is in any community. Informants complain of the frequency of adultery. It should be noted that public opinion seems to condemn it strongly, and men who have discovered their wives being unfaithful usually send them away. The adulterer has to pay a heavy fine, assuming that he does not move away. The usual figure given for a fine was two cattle and a big pig, though in practice the fine would be smaller; in one case in 1948 it was 200 escudos (£2 10s.) and a pig. The word for the man who commits adultery with one's wife, or who marries one's ex-wife, is *tjikwelume* (he of jealousy) a word already referred to in the account of the kinship terminology. There is a rule against eating with him and if one goes to his funeral it is said that one's own death will soon follow. There is a similar rule against a woman eating with the wife of a man with whom she has committed adultery.

[18] For a detailed discussion of this concept, see Hastings, pp. 111–25. It is not nowadays believed that it afflicts people guilty of pre-marital sexual relations.

Marriages may also be ended by the wife leaving her husband. This may be the consequence of quarrels; however at times a woman may just run off without any apparent reason. Her husband may go to her kin and bring her back or may just get married again—such an episode may occur after many years of a marriage which has previously appeared happy. People who have been married previously can be married again according to the pattern described previously. Middle-aged and elderly people would leave out the festivities and would just have the meal together, or simply count themselves as married by the payment of the bridewealth.

There does exist a formal ceremony of divorce in which maize flour is smeared on the upper part of the face by the husband, and this will take place in the presence of representatives of the wife's kin. A man will do this when his wife has shown herself disrespectful to him or has quarrelled with his kin or her co-wife. As the Ovimbundu regard marriage as being for the procreation of children, a barren wife should be, they say, sent away but often in practice this is not done, if the wife is otherwise satisfactory.

Legally, the Portuguese administration recognizes both the customary marriage and the Catholic marriage ceremony. The Catholic missions report to the post people who, having been married in church, then make customary marriages, and these may be subjected to such sanctions as being sent to contract labour. The Protestant church marriages are not apparently legally recognized but they are subject to the authority of the Protestant church courts which grant divorces on certain grounds. The *chefe de posto* on his annual visit to take the check on the census may get angry with polygynists, but in fact no very effective administrative action exists with regard to indigenous marriage.

The motives given for polygynous marriage are the desire to have many children and (in the case of a chief) the need to have cooks to provide hospitality for guests. Large-scale polygyny is thought to be rather funny; I was told, as something amusing, that the former chief Mbati had 17 wives. Kafelo, the former chief of Gumba, had 6 wives, the highest number of continuing polygynous marriages I found. In Epalanga out of

17 married men, 5 were polygynists. It is a common practice for a man with two wives to keep one in one village, another in another. Relations between co-wives are expected to be somewhat strained, as the very word for co-wife, *osepekai* (she of the jealousy of women) indicates. When I asked if a woman would help a co-wife who had run short of grain I was told that she would not help but would jeer at the other woman. There is no defined division of duties between wives in a polygynous household. It is interesting to note that the missions are not criticized for imposing monogamy—indeed the Catholic catechist of Epalanga thought he had found a good argument against the Protestants by accusing them sincerely but inaccurately of allowing polygynous marriages. The idea of Catholic marriage as indissoluble is difficult for many Ovimbundu converts.

While the most common form of household is that of the elementary family, the fact that not all widows or divorcées are absorbed into such households leads to the appearance of households under women heads of which there were 9 (out of a total of 36) in Epalanga. Such a household may be two-(mother, children) or three-generation groups (grandmother, daughter(s), grandchildren). Of these 9 households 2 were composed of a grandmother, who was effective head of the household, her children, and the children of a daughter; 1 was similarly composed but with the grandmother rather pushed into the background as in households with male heads; 3 were composed of women and their own child, or children; 1 was composed of a woman and a grandchild; and 2 consisted of women living alone. The adolescent sons of such a household will tend to become associated with the house of some male kinsman, probably a mother's brother. It is not always clear to what extent individuals associated with a particular household in fact participate in its activities. Thus it is not infrequent to find the elderly mother of the husband or wife living in a hut of her own behind the main hut or huts of the household, and in Epalanga there were four of these attached mothers. They do not exercise any authority over their sons, or sons-in-law.[19]

[19] Tumbu, the mother of Maria, the wife of Paulo (24), and of Jaime (19) lived in a hut near both households, and it would have been difficult to say to which she was attached, to her son's, or her son-in-law's.

At the other end of the age-scale it is not easy always to tell to what household a child is attached. Small children may often eat with kin other than their own parents if they like them and thus share in the lives of two households. Children and adolescents may go on visits to kin and this may lead to permanent residence. This familiarity with other households is not confined to children. Although, as has been stated, eating with one's wife is the usual practice, it is by no means uncommon to see two or more men eating together, either because the wife of one of them is away or simply to be sociable.

This right of children to move about, coupled with such other factors[20] as the relatively high divorce rate, tends to bring about quite a high proportion of children who live with kin other than their own parents. Out of 70 under 20's in Epalanga (out of a total population of 148), 34 had both parents living in Epalanga,[21] 23 had one parent living in Epalanga and 13 had neither parent living in Epalanga. Of the 23 who had only one parent living in Epalanga, 7 lived with their father and 16 with their mother. Those 7 living with their father were all over 14, thus confirming the norm given by informants that young children on the death of the mother go to their mother's kin until they 'have sense', that is, are about 12 or 13, when they return to their father. Of the 13 who were living with neither parent, 2 (boys) were living with a cross-cousin (father's sister's son, for whom the term 'father' can be used), 1 (boy) with a patrilateral 'father,' 2 (1 girl, 1 small boy) with a mother's mother, 4 (3 boys, 1 girl) with a sister's husband, 1 (boy) with a paternal half-brother, 1 with a fiancé's father, 1 (boy) with a mother's brother, and on 1 (girl) I have no information.

These figures are too small to base any very strong argument on them. It is, however, notable that only 1 of the 12 children on whom information was obtained was living with a mother's brother, whereas 4 were living with a brother-in-law. This seems to conflict with statements made earlier as to the present-day trend of individuals to settle with their mother's brothers.

[20] Childs notes about the traditional system that the sending of children to stay with kin or friends for a year or two was common (pp. 104–5).

[21] This figure includes one case where although both parents lived in Epalanga they were separated.

This strong pull towards the mother's brother is, however, marked on the level of village relationships as has been already noted. It is possible that with regard to co-operation on the domestic plane the tie between a man and his wife's full or half siblings is stronger than that with his sister's children. This argument would claim that the tie created by marriage between a man and his wife's full or half siblings is one of the strongest in the Umbundu social structure, and as a further proof (albeit not quantitively assessed) may be quoted the frequency with which two households close together turn out to belong to a man and his wife's brother.

In the first section of this chapter it was argued that the high rate of preferential marriages greatly increased the number of social ties between individuals in a neighbourhood, and brought a renewal of ties with distant kin. In this section various aspects of the relationship between husband and wife have been examined. Husband and wife co-operate economically and outside working hours may pass their evenings together. In a dispute taken to the post a man is likely to take his wife as a witness. Mystically sanctioned obligations do exist between husband and wife. While the elementary family is the main domestic type, households headed by women are also found and there is a certain amount of mobility of children between households. The tie of a man with his wife's siblings, particularly when they are children, is significant for the domestic organization of households.

Marriage is indeed the pivotal institution of the Umbundu kinship system. The preferential marriages do not link descent groups to one another; rather they bring about the local concentration of kin which makes out of many vague and insecure links a strongly-woven community in which both husband and wife can live with relatives near at hand.

Of the personal relationship between husband and wife it would be impossible to say as an anthropologist has of another African people, 'Here people looked for little in marriage. A man would turn to his sixteenth cousin twice removed before he turned to his wife.'[22] A man shares with his wife his work and leisure, is linked to her by mystical obligations which are not

[22] Elenore Smith Bowen, *Return to Laughter*, London, 1954, p. 117.

ended by her death, and can rely on her testimony in a case. Even though adultery is reputedly frequent it is deplored and, as will be shown in a discussion of disputes, a man's hostility to another will be ascribed to thwarted lust for the latter's wife. The conjugal bond is the closest social relation that can exist between adults, and therefore the very type of personal enmity is provided by the adulterer or would-be adulterer.

I am here emphasizing the factors which strengthen the conjugal bond; at the end of the previous chapter I emphasized the strength which the brother-sister tie possessed under changed conditions. The balance between these two ties is to be seen in the way in which a man and his wife's brother are often next door neighbours and the best of friends. It may be suggested that this balance reflects the part-peasant part-proletarian condition of the Ovimbundu, the emergence of the conjugal family with its importance as the working team for the cultivation of cash crops, and the 'reshaping of' the brother-sister tie with the absence of husbands as labourers. It seems probable from the example of the substantial coffee-growers that had the Ovimbundu become full-time cultivators there would have been a strong trend towards isolated households and the weakening of the 'neo-matrilineal' pull which operates in the villages.

It is then the marriage tie which holds the vague, amorphous, kinship system together; it is against this vagueness that the marriage bond appears as the closest and most definite relation that can exist between two adults; and the change-over from trade to an economy based on wage-labour and cash agriculture has been accompanied by a transition from a double-descent kinship system to one in which the emergence of the elementary family co-exists with a certain pull towards matrilineal kin.

CHAPTER IX

SOCIAL CONTROL

━━━━vvvvɅɅvⱱ/ⱱ⃝ⱱ/ⱱⱱvⱱvvw━━━━

1. *Introduction*

In this chapter I shall describe and analyse three disputes
which reveal the working of social control in present-day
Umbundu society. The first dispute is between an elder of the
school and a government headman, the second is between a
traditional headman and a villager with the intervention of a
local self-styled *assimilado*[1], and the third arose from a quarrel
between an irregularly installed chief and a traditional headman.

The points which it is hoped will arise from the analysis of
the material are the disappearance or extreme weakness of the
traditional institutions of social control, the way in which the
Ovimbundu appeal to the members of the 'civilized' community
for decisions or support in cases, and how kinship ties affect the
relations between persons involved in a dispute.

2. *Guilherme and Paulo*

The parties principally involved in the first dispute were Paulo
(24. See List of Epalanga residents), the elder of the school
at Epalanga, and his cross-cousin Guilherme (see List II, p. 55),
a government headman then living in Epalanga, Francisco,
a son of the former chief Mbati and wife's brother to Paulo,
and Sapapula (10), the headman and reputed founder of
Epalanga. The sequence of the dispute is first a quarrel between
Paulo and Guilherme. Guilherme then attacks Paulo through
his wife's brother Francisco. This brings about a general attack

[1] The fact that Justino was not actually an *assimilado* is not relevant, since he
used the belief of the local people that he was.

by the people under Paulo's leadership on Guilherme's position. Guilherme counter-attacks by using his relationship with the post but finds himself forced to seek a reconciliation with the people of Epalanga.

The quarrel had begun with the proposed marriage of Anna, a step-daughter of Guilherme, and a member of his household, to Luciano, a son of the former chief Simbwyikoka and an inhabitant of the latter's village. Guilherme had no effective religious affiliation but Anna had been baptized as a Catholic, her godmother being Maria, the wife of Paulo. Luciano on the other hand was the elder of the Protestant catechetical school in Simbwyikoka village. Paulo therefore intervened to stop the marriage in accordance with the rule made by the Catholic missions against marriage with non-Catholics. Guilherme, angry at this, decided to pick on Pedro Nendi (see List II, p. 55) and Francisco Lyonjanga, sons of Mbati, and therefore wife's brothers to Paulo. Pedro Nendi had been at one time a Catholic catechist but had since been dismissed. Francisco was at the time of my arrival in Epalanga moving out of his village to settle near Pedro in a hamlet near the village. He worked as assistant to Abel Pinheiro, an African carpenter, who lived a little further along the road to Chicunda and who was employed by a white living elsewhere. Guilherme accordingly reported to the post that the two brothers had never gone to contract labour and got a policeman to come with an order for them to be brought to the post for contract labour. The policeman arrived and got Francisco, but Pedro was away visiting relatives at Nova Lisboa. Francisco then claimed that he was in fact employed by a white and was therefore exempt from contract labour. At that time Antonio Pires, an African priest from the *Missão Católica de Bimbe*, was visiting Epalanga as part of a tour through the villages. Accordingly, on the morning of the 16th January 1956, Francisco came to my house where the priest had been breakfasting with me, and stated his case. This action brought the dispute between Guilherme and Paulo for the first time within the sphere of a representative of the civilized community. The priest told Francisco to get a letter from his employer to the post. Francisco duly arrived at the post with a letter, but forgot to bring his pass[2] and was sent to contract labour. The *chefe* apparently informed his employer that he could get other carpenters from the post.

Paulo, then acting in his official capacity as elder of the school, had intervened in a projected marriage in which Guilherme had received the bridewealth. Guilherme, acting in his official capacity, had attacked Paulo's wife's brothers Francisco and Pedro. The dispute had now been brought within the sphere of the mission (as represented by the priest Antonio Pires) and of the administration which had ordered the recruitment of the two men. The conflict between Guilherme and Paulo was now to widen out to include several other people.

On the 21st January the strain between Guilherme and Paulo showed itself again in violent quarrelling, from which I learnt about the broken engagement of Anna. Paulo said that he would refer the matter to Antonio Pires when the priest came back.

On the morning of the 24th the question was brought before Antonio Pires, the catechist Pedro Chiquete Santos (35), Paulo, and Guilherme all speaking in turn. Then other people raised their grievances. Sapapula declared that Guilherme was the enemy of everybody in the village. A man called Kasosi (7), a sister's son of Wasuka (15), stepped forward to claim that Guilherme had attacked him and injured him. Apparently Guilherme, while having illicit rum in his own house, had beaten up Kasosi for possessing rum. Both Maria, Paulo's wife, and Nahoka, Sapapula's wife, joined in the argument. The only man who seemed in any way favourable to Guilherme was Kapapelo (see List II, p. 55), a mother's brother of his, who was also a 'brother' of Lusase (see List II, p. 55). Antonio Pires came down heavily against Guilherme, at which the latter declared that he owed obedience only to the post and ran off.

Towards the end of the argument Luciano (the former fiancé of Anna) and Jeremias (the Protestant catechist from Simbwyi-koka) came to the priest to ask for the repayment of the bride-wealth.

On the 25th Lusase, the chief of Gumba, happened to visit

---

[2] The legal obligation for natives to possess passes is not enforced with the zeal which applies in South Africa.

Epalanga. Told what had happened, he said that he would keep out of it, and that he had advised Guilherme to live elsewhere. In the afternoon of the same day, as heavy rain was falling, a number of people ran up and bounded on to my veranda. These included Anna, another girl (I think a sister of hers) both rather frightened, Simbwyikoka, Luciano, Paulo and some others. Anna said that Simbwyikoka was a sorcerer[3] and would kill her, and sooner than be killed by sorcery she would jump in the river. Simbwyikoka and Luciano had come to Epalanga to try and recover the 250 escudos which had been paid over in bridewealth. The catechist tried to intervene saying 'The catechist is the chief[4] of everybody in the village', but nobody paid any attention to him. Eventually, as the girl continued to threaten to jump in the river, I contributed 200 escudos, and so those involved left satisfied.

Early the following day I heard that Guilherme had returned from the post with two policemen to arrest various people. Those arrested were Sapapula, his cross-cousins Epalata (5), and Wasuka, and the latter's son Kuseka, Kasosi, Paulo, Pedro the catechist, Bartolomeu (32), Paulo's assistant in school matters, and his son Eugenio. Eugenio and Kuseka were arrested for not paying taxes and their fathers were arrested presumably for their supposed responsibility. Epalata was arrested for a similar alleged offence on the part of one of his sons, who was away as a labourer.

When I came to Guilherme's house a lengthy wrangle was going on from which I select some themes. Guilherme denied that he had planned to burn the catechetical school, the anthropologist's house, and his own house. (These charges were almost certainly invented.)

Paulo said that he had baptized a dying son of Guilherme, who, despite this, had not shown him any respect. He also denied that he had committed adultery with Guilherme's wife. (This would in any case be most unlikely owing to Paulo's blindness, resulting from an eye disease.)

Sapapula declared angrily: 'I gave Guilherme land here but

[3] This accusation was regarded simply as the product of fear and nothing more was heard of it.

[4] He used the word applied to chiefs of Gumba and other sub-chiefdom.

131

Guilherme isn't grateful'—(then to Guilherme) 'I did no harm, I gave you everything, and you beat me.' This arguing eventually died down.

A little later another quarrel sprang up between Wasuka, and Kapapelo, Guilherme's mother's brother and witness. Wasuka declared that Kapapelo had committed adultery with his wife and must be killed. Kapapelo indignantly denied this.

The same day the catechist went to the mission to find the priest Antonio Pires to ask him to support the case against Guilherme. He returned to say that Padre Pires had been moved to the Bailundo Mission, but that he had been given a letter from the mission to the post setting out the case.

Guilherme in the evening came to my house to pay back the 200 escudos which I had paid to Simbwyikoka for the bride-wealth given for Anna. He had raised the 200 escudos from Paulo (his cross-cousin) and from Bartolomeu (his 'brother'), both of whom were under arrest (although free to walk about the village) through Guilherme's actions.

The following day (27th January) the policeman moved off with Guilherme and the others, Bartolomeu, Eugenio, Epalata, Wasuka, Kuseka, Kasosi, Paulo, Pedro Chiquete Santos (the catechist) and Sapapula.

About noon the next day I found that Paulo and the catechist had returned to Epalanga and heard from them what had happened. On the way Guilherme had declared that his violent temper was to blame in having so many people arrested, apologized, and promised to go to another village. He pulled out a knife and threatened to commit suicide if this proposal was not accepted. This appeal was directed mainly to the catechist, and was reinforced by Guilherme's wife, who also threatened suicide and appealed to the catechist's feelings by pointing out that she had had two of her children baptized. This was accepted, and accordingly all turned back to the village except for Guilherme, Bartolomeu, his son Eugenio, and Wasuka's son Kuseka. Eugenio and Kuseka had been arrested for not paying taxes, a matter of more interest to the *chefe* than the village brawl for which the others had been arrested. Eugenio and Kuseka were considered by the *chefe* not to be yet old enough for payment of tax, and Guilherme produced some story to explain the non-appearance of the others which satisfied the *chefe*.

The catechist was somewhat criticized for not having pushed on with the case, and thereby perhaps getting Guilherme landed in jail. Guilherme did move out of the village in February and settled near the outskirts of the Protestant village of Kalungwengwe. Kapapelo also set about moving out of Epalanga.

In the conflict which has just been described, there are three disputes, the question of the bridewealth which involved Luciano, Simbwyikoka, Guilherme, and the anthropologist, the quarrel between Paulo and Guilherme, and the subsequent uprising against Guilherme which takes its signal from Paulo's reference of the dispute to the priest.

The question of bridewealth repayment is subordinate to, indeed enclosed within, the main dispute. It does illustrate one point central to the problem of Umbundu social control, the absence of any court machinery. Jeremias and Luciano had tried to recover it by appealing to the priest; later Luciano and Simbwyikoka attempted to get it back by coming and demanding it, that is by self-help. Another extremely significant aspect of the social structure is revealed by this 'enclosed' case. Guilherme after a bitter dispute with Paulo which has ended in the arrest of Paulo and Bartolomeu borrows 200 escudos from them as a kinsman. This indicates that kinship ties can survive and function despite a quarrel which they do not check or prevent, a point which will be developed later in an examination of how kinship affects and is affected by a dispute.

The conflict cannot be viewed as simply a dispute between individuals, nor as a dispute between the holders of opposed roles. Guilherme was generally regarded as lacking 'sense' (*olondunge*), the quality, greatly admired by the Ovimbundu, of good judgement and decent social behaviour, and he confessed himself to be at fault. Yet he could not have acted in the way he did unless he had been a government headman, nor would the uprising against him have taken the form it did had he not held an office dependent on the post. There is, however, no necessary conflict between a government headman and the catechist or elder of the school in the sense that there is no sphere where their duties overlap and where they must compete.

The roles of government headmen and of officials of the school are complementary. It is through the chief and the government headman that the Ovimbundu pay their taxes and fines, are recruited as contract labourers and are called to road service, are arrested for crimes and misdemeanours and are entered on official records. It is through the catechists and elders of the school that the Ovimbundu find the expression of village unity by which at the same time they are linked to the whites and to the rest of the world on the religious level. The missions bring the Ovimbundu closer to the whites than does the administration, without the administration's predominant interest in making demands.[5]

While at the level of the total Angolan political system the administration is more powerful than the missions, the position of the catechist or elder of the school is stronger at the local level because the catechist and the elder represent the catechetical school which is the only social grouping existing on a village basis, whereas the government headman in fact represents no social group but is simply an executant of the orders of the *chefe*. Hence the catechist owing to this representative role and to his contact with the mission (which is much closer than that of the government headman) can lead the people and invoke the aid of the mission against abuses on the part of chiefs or government headmen. This would not be the case if the post gave firm backing to its local agents and turned a deaf ear to communications from the missions. Opposition to an overbearing government headman is then likely to be led by the leaders of the 'school', who can count on the backing of the mission, if they have a good case, to intervene for them at the post. The relative importance in a village of the catechist and elder of the school varies according to such factors as personality. The way in which the catechist was ignored when he tried to intervene in the dispute over the bridewealth shows that the catechist cannot claim authority in disputes as a matter of course.

[5] The missions impose fees and a yearly levy on their adherents which are small compared to the official taxes.

The transformation of the dispute between Guilherme and Paulo into what amounted to both a trial of, and an uprising against, the government headman is not purely accidental but is a natural consequence of the principle latent in the social organization by which the 'school' leaders complement and can check the chief and government headman.

The case also indicates the limited nature of their roles. Both Paulo (by preventing Anna's marriage) and Guilherme (by getting Francisco sent to contract labour) can strike at the other through the lawful exercise of their authority; any real attack on the other's position involves an appeal to either mission or post, and hence brings about a trial of some sort. Guilherme finding that the quasi-trial before the priest went against him, tried to bring the case before the post, but realizing that this also was likely to go against him came to terms with his enemies. That is, any determined attempt to solve a dispute is likely to involve at least the threat of a reference to the post or the mission.

The power of the priest to intervene in the actions of the agents of the post is limited. Thus Antonio Pires did not intervene in the case of Francisco but advised him to get a letter from his employer. It is, however, notable that the missionaries are not simply appealed to by Catholics. Protestants like Jeremias and Luciano, and pagans like Kasosi and Sapapula, were ready to appeal to the priest although the initiative came from Paulo. That this is so is a convincing argument for the claim which has been made that the catechetical school represents the whole village, although it could also be claimed that it reflects rather an aspect of 'civilized'-native relations in the total Angolan system, clientship, as the typical form of relations between the two groups, with the missions being the patrons *par excellence* to whom all natives are at least potentially clients. The general well-being of all natives is the concern of the missions, who are therefore liable to be appealed to in such cases as this.

In particular cases where there is another patron to appeal to his aid will be sought. This patron-client situation will crop up again in the account of subsequent disputes. Its origin historically lies in the history of attitudes to employees and to servants in Portugal and Angola;[6] sociologically it reflects the lack of any system of bureaucratic administration at the local level and the isolation of the *chefes* from the people. The uncertainties of taking a case to the post are such that it is thought desirable to have some backing (such as the letter the catechist got from the mission) from a representative of the 'civilized' community and in the absence of any other 'civilized' person the mission becomes the patron of all natives, whatever their religious allegiance.

The importance of this case, then, is its illustration of what may happen in a conflict between a catechist or elder of the school and a government headman. The limited nature of their powers, and the fact that their roles are not competitive, make a conflict between them, so long as it is not extended to pull in other people, necessarily confined to indirect attacks. If either party wishes to bring down the other he must appeal to the post or to the mission. The government headman can pull people in by accusing them at the post of not paying taxes or creating a disturbance, or by recommending them for contract labour. His position is not so strong as his dependence on the post might suggest, since the intervention of the mission, at the request of the villagers, can bring him down.

Within this main 'political' dispute is the quarrel over bridewealth, which is illuminating both in indicating the absence of legal mechanisms at the village level, and in showing how kinship ties continue to function at the height of a bitter quarrel. Both these points will be noticed again in the accounts of later disputes.

3. *Kapapelo and Sapapula*

The next case involved Sapapula and Kapapelo and was again to end in an averted appeal to the *chefe de posto*. On the 21st of February Sapapula, Sahuke (see List II, p. 56), Wasuka, Luanga (21), and others went from Epalanga to the house of Justino, who had called them there to settle a dispute. Justino

---

[6] An inhabitant of Lisbon, wishing to emigrate to Canada, wooed the maid of a former official of the British Embassy. Discovering that this would get him nowhere, he transferred his affections to the maid of one of the staff of the American Embassy. The implications are interesting.

was a man of fifty or more, who lived in Portuguese style making money from coffee and other crops. He claimed to be an *assimilado* (African with the status of a Portuguese citizen) but in actual fact he was not one. He had employed a man called Kusumula, who lived in Epalanga and was the brother of Kapapelo's wife.

To appreciate the point of Justino's complaint, it is necessary to explain the significance of certain terms indicative of ethnic and social status. Otjimbundu is the singular of Ovimbundu, a people defined by the use of the Umbundu language. It is also used to refer to any black person (thus I was often asked whether there were Ovimbundu [i.e. Africans] in England), and is therefore equivalent to the Portuguese *preto* (black), which when used of a person has a rather pejorative sense like 'native' in other parts of Africa. Livingstone, writing a hundred years ago, remarks of one area in Angola: 'The people under him (the chief) are divided into a number of classes. . . . They are also divided into gentlemen and little gentlemen, and, though quite black, speak of themselves as white men and of the others, who may not wear shoes, as "blacks".'[7] Justino's complaint was that Sapapula had referred to him as a *preto qualquer* or in Umbundu (Sapapula did not speak Portuguese), *otjimbundu tjango*, a mere black.

Justino delivered a speech when the people from Epalanga had settled on the veranda of his house in which he declared with much force that he was not an Otjimbundu '*Ame sitjimbunduko.*' This accusation was based on information given him by Kusumula, who alleged that Sapapula had said to government headmen that Kusumula could be recruited for road work, as he worked not for a white (a term applied also to *assimilados*) but for a mere black.

I give the main lines of the ensuing argument. Sapapula denied that he had called Justino a black. Kusumula claimed that Sapapula was always picking on him. Sapapula declared that he had founded the village, and that Kusumula wanted to break it up. Kapapelo said that he had at one time given medicine to a girl and Sapapula had told Jaime to kill him because he might have seduced her. Kutenga Lusase, the chief

---

[7] Livingstone, *Missionary Travels and Researches*, p. 411.

of Gumba who had also turned up, intervened and denounced Kusumula for not wishing to work for the post, and then brought the case back to Sapapula's alleged slander of Justino. The latter intervened again here to say that he had been slandered. Sapapula, by now very excited, denied this and said that Kusumula and Kapapelo wanted to break up the village. This was followed by three people trying to talk at once. Justino strolled round to the back of his house. Sapapula and Kapapelo wrangled.

Justino was not the only person to find this tedious. Paulo suggested that we should go. Kapapelo complained that Saviel, a sister's son of Sapapula, had made advances to his wife. Sapapula continued to declare that Kapapelo must not break up the village. Kutenga Lusase criticized Kapapelo for not working for the post. Gonçalve (18) intervened to refer back to the visit of the priest, Antonio Pires, and said that he had left with the words (i.e. he had come to a decision). Gonçalve was a pagan. The wrangling continued until Justino returned, told Sapapula not to insult him again and not to be angry with Kusumula. Sapapula said that Kusumula had left the village (Epalanga) and so would not be needed for the post again (that is, Sapapula would not be any longer responsible for him), and that he had never been angry with Kapapelo. Nahoka, Sapapula's wife, said that Kapapelo was not *ukwafeka* 'a man of the country'. Justino then dismissed the gathering, telling Sapapula to buy a bottle of wine for the elders who had come with him.

Kapapelo and Kusumula were not connected with the post as Guilherme was, nor with the mission as Paulo was. Kusumula was the employee of Justino and had thus an opportunity to appeal to him by accusing Sapapula of denying his status. It is not particularly significant whether Sapapula had actually said this or not. The accusation is important since it is a reflection of a common Umbundu way of attacking one's enemies, by accusing them of some offence against a 'civilized' person. Thus, to refer back to the earlier dispute between Paulo and Guilherme, the latter found it necessary to deny that he had planned to set fire to the catechetical school and the anthropologist's house, charges which were intended to weigh heavily with the *chefe*. Hence, when a quarrel between natives comes to a civilized person, it is likely that the details will be re-organized to gain his attention and support.

It is also notable that Sapapula was ready to accept Justino's right to hold a case on the matter. The acceptance and even readiness (as appears later) on Sapapula's part that Justino should hear cases is partly again a result of the lack of any legal machinery on the village level, partly an aspect of the 'patron-client' situation which has so often marked 'civilized'-native relations in Angola. No doubt much in Justino's behaviour arose from the taste he showed at times for settling cases, which led to a certain number of local cases being referred to him, and his readiness to settle them may not have been particularly common among *assimilados*.

Much of the actual case consisted of accusations and counter-accusations between Sapapula and Kapapelo with other people intervening. There is a kind of attempt to establish a balance of wrongs, Kusumula claiming that Sapapula was always picking on him when there was a call for labour from the post, Kapapelo accusing Sapapula of inciting Jaime to kill him and Sapapula's sister's son Saviel of planning to seduce his wife. Sapapula had accused Kusumula and Kapapelo of trying to break the village. Lusase intervened rather against Kusumula and Kapapelo, who was his 'brother'. As previously, the demands of the post for labour are regarded as being used by their local executants in a discriminating way.

On the evening of the same day, as I was calling round the village, I found Kapapelo at the door of Sapapula's kitchen. Apparently he had arrived drunk and had threatened to kill himself. Sapapula was greatly enraged at this, as were his women folk, Nahoka, his wife, Wumba, his daughter, and Nayangu, his 'sister', who vigorously abused Kapapelo. They warned Sapapula not to accept food from Kapapelo, lest the latter use it as a means of sorcery. Kapapelo complained that Nahoka had called him a slave thus expanding the hint contained in her previous enigmatic remark that Kapapelo was not a man of the country.

On the next day, Wednesday the 22nd, Sapapula had intended to go again to Justino's to settle his case with Kapapelo, but there was a funeral to which a large number of people went.

Moreover, Justino did not want to bother any more with the case, and said that anybody who went on with it was just vindictive. It had been proposed to hold a moot at Sapapula's house, but this was impracticable as Kapapelo would not come. Accordingly, on the afternoon of the 23rd February, a number of people gathered at Kapapelo's house. The gathering at first consisted of Sapapula, Sahuke, and Kafelo (the former chief) who sat close together joined by the anthropologist and his interpreter Pedro Chimbalanya Epalanga, two men from Menga, one of them a son of Sapapula, Nahoka, Nayangu, and Wumba respectively (as previously mentioned), Sapapula's wife, 'sister', and daughter, Lusase the *de facto* chief of Gumba, Ngombe the Mwekalia at his court, Alexandro a son of Mwehombo, temporarily visiting Epalanga, and four people from Ndjoleya's end of Epalanga, Augusto (25) (grandson-in-law of Sapapula), Costa (26), Ferreira (28), and Filemeno, who later moved to Belem. Other people turned up later, including Ndjoleya (30) himself. My point in quoting these names is to show that the crowd which turned up to the moot was not composed either of Sapapula's kin or of his co-villagers as exclusive groups.

Lusase was not received with any great respect, but bowed low to Kafelo. Ngombe explained that he had been invited as a guest.[8] Sapapula explained to Ngombe what had happened at Justino's. By this time Epalata, Luanga, Paulo, and Wasuka had arrived. Sapapula alleged that Kapapelo had wanted to seduce Nahoka, but that she had refused, and that Kapapelo had then wanted to kill him so that he could then obtain Nahoka. The conversation between Kapapelo and Nahoka had been in the woods so that he had no witnesses. Sapapula, who was now very angry, finished his speech by declaring that he had given land to Kapapelo. Meanwhile more people arrived.

Ngombe now spoke discussing the evidence and summing up very much against Kapapelo. Lusase spoke, avoiding the

[8] On another occasion, three elders from Gumba (one of them Simbwyikoka) were invited to Chicunda to arbitrate a case. Ngombe's appearance here in fact was not significant, except perhaps as showing the discrepancy between ideas about cases and the reality.

question of Kapapelo's intention towards Nahoka, but criticized Kapapelo for reopening his quarrel with Sapapula. Kapapelo (who did not strike me as particularly intelligent) was wandering about more or less ignoring the criticisms which had been made of him, which greatly annoyed the assembly. At length, Kapapelo, urged to speak by Lusase, did so.

Kapapelo stated that he had committed adultery with Nahoka, Sapapula's wife, and asked to be fined for adultery. This created a fresh uproar. Nahoka got up and said that the question was within the competence of Lusase since he and not Kafelo was now the chief. She denied that she had committed adultery. As evidence against this, she pointed out that Kapapelo's wife had visited her house to eat mush, and that Kapapelo's conduct when he came to Sapapula's kitchen showed that she had not committed adultery. Antonio Kasoma (see List II, p. 55) said that it was necessary to decide how much Kapapelo should pay.

Kapapelo's wife joined in to support her husband's confession, saying that Kapapelo had given Nahoka soap. Sapapula declared that Kapapelo was worthless, and had received everything he had from Sapapula. Some people called on Kapapelo to work sorcery. Kafelo suggested that Kapapelo should pay 150 escudos (£1. 17s. 6d.). The meeting now broke up, some people saying that the post should be informed and that Kapapelo had (illicit) rum in his house. One of the Menga men said that in the past even attempted seductions were punished. Sapapula demanded a payment of 500 escudos or a big pig, for Kapapelo's offences of not showing respect to Sapapula, and attempting adultery. He seemed more inclined, however, to take the case to the post, since (he claimed) Kapapelo was threatening to kill him. Kapapelo refused to pay.

The argument now swirled round, Kapapelo wavering between paying and not paying, Sapapula wavering between going to the post and being ready to accept a fine. Kafelo and Lusase both favoured a payment. People said that Guilherme was responsible for this. Paulo, Kusumula and Ndjoleya all urged Kapapelo to pay. Sapapula had now moved off, and was eventually followed by everybody else. Various wrangles continued over the question of paying a fine or having recourse to the post. Somebody said to me 'Lusase wants a fine to be paid so that he can get something from it' (the chief traditionally having a right to commission on a fine paid in a dispute which he had settled). Eventually the dispute did not go to the post, as Kapapelo paid a fine, and the matter dropped.

A great deal of detail has been given here, but it can be shown that consistencies can be extracted from what seems complete confusion.

Kapapelo had, no doubt, as was said, under the influence of drink, decided to carry on his conflict with Sapapula after the gathering at Justino's and had arrived at Sapapula's threatening to commit suicide. The threat of suicide was here used as Guilherme had used it to put an opponent in a difficult position, but it infuriated Sapapula, who decided that he must try and get another hearing. He therefore turned again to Justino, although the latter had previously decided against him; thus implying that even a possibly unfavourable judge is acceptable, rather than let a squabble continue indefinitely.

Eventually, owing to Justino's refusal to hear the case, what I have called a 'moot' was got together, a body which lacked any deciding, dominating figure, but represented the local community. This became concerned with the question of the relation of Kapapelo and Sapapula as affected by the action of Kapapelo in respect of Sapapula's wife Nahoka. As has been mentioned in the chapter on marriage, the relation between a man and his wife's lover is one of mystically manifested hostility. Sapapula by accusing Kapapelo of desiring to seduce his wife was indicating a very serious state of hostility between the two men; and one can only explain Kapapelo's confession to something of which he was not guilty as a mark of his hostility to Sapapula. Kapapelo was accused by Sapapula of attempting to do him a grievous wrong, and Kapapelo claimed that he had in fact done this wrong. Nahoka denied that she had wronged her husband, and produced evidence of her assertion. Before considering her arguments, it must be noted what were the interests of the other people involved in the case.

It might be suggested that Kafelo, Lusase, and Ngombe had to some extent the function of judges or at least arbitrators, and Sapapula had indeed invited Ngombe to give his opinion (I do not know how Kafelo and Lusase came to hear of the case). In practice, their role was that of any other spectator in trying to bring about a settlement, although a chief has, as was noted, the right to a commission on any indemnification. The right of spectators to intervene is not based on any particular relationship to those involved nor on any reputation for wisdom. There is in fact no organized routine for determining who may and who must turn up and who may and who must speak. Spectators and speakers are simply members of the neighbourhood community, some related to Sapapula, some simply fellow-villagers, and it is natural that in present Umbundu society, lacking clearly-defined social groups, the crowd that assembles on such an occasion should look like a chance gathering. Its lack of recognized procedure, of accepted leadership, and of specific criteria of recruitment are all typical of the neighbourhood community among the contemporary Ovimbundu.

Despite the 'unorganized' character of this gathering, there exists evidently a set of generally accepted symbolic values, which are accepted by Christian and pagan, by young and old. Thus Nahoka claimed as evidence that she had not committed adultery her meal with Kapapelo's wife, and the latter in turn offered as evidence that adultery had been committed a statement that her husband had made a gift of soap to Nahoka. These actions provide presumptive evidence of innocence or guilt since an adulterer or adulteress may not eat under apparently mystical sanctions with the spouse of the person with whom he or she has committed adultery, and the giving of gifts by a man to a woman implies a sexual relationship. These actions were presumably recognized as convincing evidence in the days when there existed a formal court system, and continue to be recognized as such at the present day.

The nature of contemporary social relations, as being the end-product of a series of acts between individuals rather than as the content of jural norms defined by status, is also revealed in the dispute, particularly in the episode at Justino's. Sapapula does not complain that Kapapelo had not behaved as a villager should to his headman, but that he had not been grateful for having been given land. Kapapelo's complaint that Saviel, Sapapula's sister's son, had attempted to seduce his wife was,

L   143

like his accusation that Sapapula had incited Jaime to kill him, an attempt to portray himself not as an ungrateful recipient of Sapapula's goodness but a much suffering victim of his malevolence.

Although the moot reflects the existing social structure and values there are occasional reminiscences of the former social system. Thus Ngombe seems to have been acting according to a traditional but non-effective pattern in giving a long, judicial, summing up, which had no practical effect. Again, when Sapapula accused Kapapelo of wishing to break up the village it is probable that he was thinking of the old villages socially defined by the agnatic tie and physically enclosed by a stockade rather than the physically and socially amorphous villages of the present day. Values such as these survive in the minds of individuals when the associated social forms have disintegrated. They are brought out on occasions analogous to those in which they were formerly used, but are not nowadays decisive in the way they would have been.

The quarrel between Kapapelo and Sapapula is different from the other cases, since the meeting held to discuss it is held without the presence of a 'civilized' person and it pivots about a question of adultery or rather attempted adultery, a subject which has hitherto appeared marginally as a subject for insults. The case is held without the presence of a 'civilized' person, and this is from necessity, not from choice. Sapapula had tried to have the case heard by Justino, and Kapapelo was eventually brought to terms by Sapapula's threat to refer the matter to the post. While the moot shows us the community acting to uphold social control, such action is regarded as an unsatisfactory substitute for a decision by somebody who could, as Gonçalve said of Antonio Pires, 'leave with the words', that is, settle the case.

Adultery has previously occurred as an accusation thrown in during a squabble that has begun with something else. Thus Guilherme accused Paulo and Wasuka accused Kapapelo of adultery because they were angry with them; they were not angry with them because they thought they had committed adultery with their wives. It is parallel to the suggestions that Kapapelo was a sorcerer, an insult not an accusation. It now occurs, whether in intention as declared by Sapapula and Nahoka, as accomplished as claimed by Kapapelo, as the substance of the conflict between the two men.

To sum up, Kapapelo had originally been aligned with his kinsman Guilherme against Sapapula, who had then shown hostility to Kapapelo, and especially to his wife's brother Kusumula. The latter had counter-attacked by accusing Sapapula before Justino, and there the matter might have rested if Kapapelo had not tried to attack Sapapula again, by making the threat to commit suicide at his kitchen door. This led to the moot at which the charge of attempted adultery was made, and at which Sapapula intended to, and succeeded in, taming Kapapelo.

4. *Lusase, Sapapula, and Luanga*

In this case, individuals previously met, notably Sapapula, and Lusase reappear, this time as enemies. The principal scenes are first an attempt by a kinsman of Lusase's to recover a debt from Sapapula, secondly an attack by Lusase on Sapapula, thirdly a decision by the *chefe de posto* in favour of Sapapula, fourthly a fresh complaint to the post by Luanga against Lusase, fifthly a post decision in favour of Luanga, sixthly and finally reconciliation of Luanga and Lusase.

This chain of disputes had begun actually before the episodes mentioned in the last case. On the 19th February, Ndonga a kinsman of Lusase (whom he had helped to power), arrived in Epalanga and tied up Sapapula, as a result of the latter not paying a debt. I produced the money and for the present no more was heard of it. Lusase said that he did not know what went on in the villages, when the matter was mentioned to him.

On 13th May, Simbwyikoka, a former chief whose village was near Sapapula's, was holding a ceremony in which a bull had been killed. Sapapula had taken part in the ceremony and had been responsible for sending a leg of the bull (the chief's traditional prerogative) not to Lusase but to Kafelo, who, although he had been deposed in 1954, had the advantage over Lusase of having passed through the royal rituals, and having been elected according to traditional rules. Lusase was angry at this, turned up at the ceremony, and attacked Sapapula.

The following morning Epalanga buzzed with indignation. Gregorio, the chief of Menga, and Mandumba, Sapapula's son, had arrived at Epalanga to express their support, and Gregorio asked me[9] to write a letter to the Mission to get its support against Lusase at the post. I said that I would go to the chief's village to persuade Lusase to seek a reconciliation. The elder Wasuka, a cross-cousin of Sapapula, declared that even if Lusase offered five cattle in compensation they would not be accepted, and Sapapula's supporters portrayed him as a much injured man, repeatedly the victim of the Guilherme, Kapapelo, Lusase, Ndonga clique. My offer to go to the chief's village fell through when we heard that Lusase was now no longer there, but near, apparently at Simbwyikoka's.

I suggested that the moot should be held at Simbwyikoka's since the case had begun there; the others said 'No, let him come over here.' The crowd settled down in the open space before my house. News was then brought to us that Lusase refused to come over and insisted on the people coming to him, declaring that he ruled all, and did not obey the anthropologist but only the *chefe*. Accordingly everybody got up and walked over to Simbwyikoka's. Here we leant that Lusase had fled. Kambungo[10], an elder of Menga and kinsmen of Sapapula, declared that somebody who behaved like this could not be chief. Gregorio the chief of Menga became involved in au argument with Ndonga, who he said was responsible for installing Lusase. This Ndonga denied. This, incidentally, was the first time that I had heard that Lusase was not properly elected. As previously noted on the fall of Kafelo, Lusase had arrived at the post and announced himself as being the new chief. The Gumba people did not protest about this for fear of possible reactions from the post.

It now became known that Lusase could not be found.

[9] It may be suggested that my interventions were not in accordance with anthropological etiquette. It is difficult to see what else I could have done; it is, after all, the local custom for 'civilized' persons to provide letters of recommendation, and a refusal on my part would not have been understood.

[10] He has been mentioned in Chapter V.

People said that he had fled to the house of his sister's son Guilherme en route for the post; Gregorio now said to me that Lusase had made advances to Nahoka, trying to seduce her by saying that Sapapula was old.

On the same day Sapapula left for the post with, as his witnesses, Nahoka and Wasuka carrying a letter of recommendation from me. At the post the *chefe* took his part and told Lusase 'Sapapula is your father' and made Lusase kneel down to seek pardon. Sapapula said that he wished to move across the river into Menga, where he had formerly lived. The *chefe* told him to stay at Epalanga (because of the anthropologist's presence there), but transferred Epalanga administratively from Gumba to Chicunda. This settlement pleased the Epalanga people. It may be added that had Sapapula actually crossed over, a number of householders, including Paulo, would not have followed him.

Despite the *chefe's* acts it was not certain whether the change was to be given effect immediately or only after the *chefe's* annual visit; hence some more wrangling took place over the question of where Epalanga was situated for such purposes as the payment of fines for rum-brewing.

Luanga, who shared with Sapapula the title of Epalanga, came to my house on the night of the 27th June to ask for a letter to the *chefe de posto*. He told me that Lusase wanted to take away his title of Epalanga and send him to contract (non-voluntary) labour. I suggested that we should go together to see Lusase at his village on the following day. The next morning he decided not to go to the chief but to go straight to the post with his wife Adriana. He told me that when Lusase became chief in 1954, he and his 'brother' Mwehombo had bought the title of Epalanga (held under Kafelo by Sapapula) which they held jointly. Luanga had paid for this two pigs equal to 1,000 escudos (about £12. 10s. in British currency) and other things as well. Luanga's motive was not political power (which the present-day chief lacks and of which his ministers have even less) nor prestige, but because he would thus be exempt from contract labour. Luanga said that he did not mind going to contract labour, but insisted on having back what he had paid to Lusase. I said I would write a letter to say that he should not go to contract labour and accordingly he left for the post with my letter.

Luanga returned quite satisfied a few days later, the *chefe* having decided in his favour. Two days later he went to the chief's village to complain of Lusase's actions. With him came Bartolomeu and Paulo. Ngombe, as Mwekalia, and thereby responsible for the relations between chief and people, acted as the presiding figure, more chairman than judge, although he spoke for some time on the case. Lusase defended himself by saying that it was not he but somebody else who had recommended Luanga for contract labour. This explanation was accepted by Luanga. Bartolomeu and Paulo received small sums of money from Lusase for acting as witnesses, and later Luanga left with Lusase for another village. Here they effected the succession of a man to his father's title of Mbesi (another ministerial position). Luanga was much pleased with his share of the fee.

Not only the personalities but many of the features of previous cases reappear here. Of the ways of acting which people choose, Ndonga and Lusase use self-help, Ndonga to recover a debt, and Lusase to uphold his prestige. Against Lusase, as against Kapapelo, a moot was formed. Lusase like Guilherme insisted on his responsibility to the post alone, when the opposition seemed to be using a 'civilized' person of a different category. Final decisions are obtained by appeals to the post but the risky nature of such procedures is shown by the desire to get a letter of recommendation. Luanga believed that Lusase had got him sent to contract labour just as Francisco believed (correctly) that Guilherme had got him recruited. Ngombe as Mwekalia is more successful here as arbitrator than in the moot at Kapapelo's. Finally we see the contrast again between the survival of formal recognition in symbol of the prestige of chieftancy (the episode of the bull's leg) and its actual impotence caught between *chefe* and people. The specific issue in this dispute turns on a conflict between a chief and his people, and it shows how a chief can be defeated in the same way that the first dispute showed a government headman being defeated.

Lusase's opponents had, as previously, other means of influencing the post. Gregorio had proposed getting a letter from the mission to give Sapapula's case, and, as things worked out, it was the anthropologist who was made the 'civilized' focus for the opposition to Lusase as Antonio Pires had been made the focus of the opposition to Guilherme. Lusase, like Guilherme, reacted by saying that he owed allegiance only to the *chefe de posto*, and running off to the post.

Luanga's case shows how desire to get out of contract labour may give a new reason for taking a ministerial title, and also once again how sending someone to contract labour is regarded as a means of injuring those whom one dislikes.

I have spoken of the conflict between Lusase and Sapapula as being a conflict between a chief and his people, and this is true in so far as it shows how opposition forms against a chief and how he can be checked. It is therefore of importance as indicating the position of the chief in the contemporary social system. The people themselves interpreted the dispute as being essentially one between individuals—Lusase's behaviour was attributed to his lust for Nahoka, and Gregorio entered the dispute not as the ruler of the neighbouring chiefdom of Menga but as a friend of Sapapula. The interpretation of what is a political conflict as a quarrel between individuals may be explained as being due to the relatively limited nature of the role of chief (Lusase) and of traditional headman (Sapapula) which therefore do not predominate in the social status of the individual. (In this particular case, had I got Lusase's viewpoint he would probably have said that he was defending his dignity as chief, whereas Sapapula did not regard Lusase as being really chief.) The lack of a formal court system or even of an articulated political system at the local level has brought into desuetude the old legal and political idioms and the Ovimbundu have not yet learnt new terms from the Portuguese.

5. *Social Control and Social Structure in the Disputes*

I now return to the points mentioned at the beginning of this chapter. It is hardly necessary to underline the decayed state of the traditional system of authority. Lusase had, at the time of the quarrel between Guilherme and Paulo, expressed his intention of staying out of the dispute, just in the same way as he said, when Ndonga's action was reported to him, that he did not know what went on in the villages. That is, Lusase disclaimed any general responsibility for maintaining law and order in the sub-chiefdom. He had turned up at the case before Justino and at the moot by Kapapelo's house, when Nahoka had pointed out that it was he, and not Kafelo, who was effectively chief. The very fact that such a remark could be made indicates a weakness in Lusase's position, and his lack of authority is further illustrated by his being but one of a crowd of would-be conciliators.

It was, indeed, Lusase's position with relation to Kafelo that brought about his quarrel with Sapapula. Lusase, on meeting Kafelo at Kapapelo's, had bowed to him, and must have been uneasily aware that public opinion held that Kafelo 'had finished', had completed the cycle of chiefly rites, whereas Lusase was just 'the *chefe de posto's* boy'. It is unlikely that there would be among the Ovimbundu developed forms of the situation reported from some colonial areas by which one person acts as chief or headman *vis-à-vis* the government while another is the real chief or headman with effective power over the people, if only because so much of the content of chieftancy today is simply post work. Yet a chief differs from a government headman precisely because of the surviving prestige which clings to the capital village, the skulls of the dead chiefs, the titled ministers, and the drums, and it was such an expression of prestige which Sapapula gave to Kafelo and denied to Lusase. Not surprisingly Lusase reacted to this sharp evidence of the weakness of his position. In acting as he did, he made things worse; since he lacked any local means of imposing his will by force, or mobilizing moral support, he had to fall back on the post.

This weakening of the chieftancy is, of course, only part of the general disintegration of the old social system. Sapapula, in personality and prestige, was the equal of any traditional head-man in the neighbourhood, and was consulted by the chief and government headmen when fines or roadworkers were required from Epalanga. Yet it was Paulo and not Sapapula who launched the attack on Guilherme, an attack speedily supported

by other villagers. Nor does residence in a village or sub-chief-dom compel or limit participation in a dispute. Neither Ndjoleya nor any of his kin participated in the dispute between Paulo and Guilherme. Gregorio came from Menga to support his friend Sapapula against Lusase, acting as a private individual, and not as the chief of Menga intervening in the internal politics of a neighbouring sub-chiefdom.

The social institutions participated in exclusively by Ovimbundu (i.e. the system of kinship and marriage and the local organization) do not provide machinery for resolving disputes. Therefore, binding decisions must be obtained from a representative of the 'civilized' society, and much importance attaches to setting out the details of the case in such a way as to gain the interest of this representative. It would seem likely from this that all cases will pass into the hands of the *chefe*, and that those 'natives' who are most closely linked to the post—the chief and the government headmen—will therefore be the most influential people in indigenous society. In fact, as the disputes show, this does not happen. Cases are taken to other 'civilized' persons—the priest Antonio Pires and the *soi-disant assimilado* Justino—and Lusase, instead of making up on the bureaucratic roundabouts what he has lost on the traditional swings, falls heavily off both.

The willingness of villagers to submit their cases to Justino and the mission rather than to the post is a result of the much closer personal contact which exists with them, and their lack of direct punitive sanctions. Any case referred to the *chefe* is thought liable to produce uncertain consequences. It was because of this that the people of Gumba did not dare to complain to the post about Lusase's usurpation; for this reason, too, Guilherme, knowing the *chefe* trusted him no more than any other native, sought reconciliation before getting to the post. The chief and government headman neither enjoy official confidence nor control access to the post.

On the level of the total Angolan society the State is obviously more powerful than the Church. On the local level the chief and government headmen have more executive power[11]

---

[11] The capacity to give orders backed by force; but this only applies to orders received from the post.

than the catechists and 'elders of the school'; yet the weakness of the agents of the post before a local opposition led, not by such traditional figures as Kafelo and Sapapula, but by the school functionaries, has been demonstrated. The post accepts intervention by the mission in supporting disputants, and the mission is ready to help not only its disputants but any native who has a strong case—that is, it has a generalized relation of patronage to all natives.[12] Hence, since in a serious dispute people look round for a 'civilized' patron, the mission is the one most likely to be appealed to, and these appeals usually go through its local agents.

While the symbiosis of two societies, one ruling, the other ruled, is a common feature of modern Africa, the extremely limited nature of the role delegated by the administration to the native authority, the 'patron-client' tie linking 'civilized' persons to the natives, and the opportunity given to patrons to intervene in cases before the *chefe*, seem to be distinctive features of Portuguese colonization.[13]

The third aspect of the social structure mentioned in the introductory section was the role in disputes of kinship ties. It has been earlier noted that Sapapula's supporters regarded him as a victim of a concerted alliance by Guilherme, Kapapelo, Lusase, and Ndonga. In fact Lusase had avoided getting involved in the dispute between Guilherme and Paulo, had supported Sapapula against Kapapelo, and had disclaimed responsibility for Ndonga's act. The present social structure is not one in which groups of kin habitually co-operate;[14] and it is possible that this belief in a coalition against Sapapula reflects memories of the old social structure.

Kinship ties between individuals seem neither to restrain them from quarrelling nor to be liable to permanent disruption as a result of quarrels. By August 1956 Kasosi was once again

[12] It is felt in administrative circles that the advancement of the African is mainly the responsibility of the missions.

[13] Anybody who knows the Portuguese well will acknowledge the importance given to personal influence (*cunha*) and the lack of esteem for bureaucratic (in the Weberian sense) procedures.

[14] See Chapters IV and VII for details on the kinship cores and on general aspects of kinship. The support which Sapapula received was not confined to his own kinship core—thus Gregorio who enthusiastically supported Sapapula was not even a kinsman.

on good terms with Guilherme, who was a 'father' of his, and even earlier in June part of the celebrations which marked the marriage of Paulo's son Jose to Pungu, a girl from Namba, whose mother had at one time been married to Kapapelo, took place at the latter's house. Most strikingly of all, as has been noted, Guilherme could borrow money from Bartolomeu and Paulo at the height of their quarrel. The kinship bond exists outside of and, it might be said, at a deeper level than, the quarrel, and the rebukes hurled at an adversary reflect this. Paulo did not complain that Guilherme was a bad cross-cousin; instead he complained that Guilherme was not grateful to him for having baptized his dying child. The motive for co-operation or conflict in everyday life is to be found not in the tracing of genealogies but in the tally of reciprocal services and grievances between two individuals.

It may be claimed that this portrait of the kinship system which emerges from the disputes as being loosely structured and lacking defined obligations, but providing an underlying continuity, is very similar to that given in Chapter VII, which was based on questioning and the observation of everyday life.

The significance of the conjugal bond appears both positively in the way Luanga and Sapapula both take their wives to the post as witnesses, and negatively in the way the hostility of Kapapelo and Lusase to Sapapula is interpreted as being inspired by lust for his wife. Even the accusations of adultery so readily hurled about in disputes reflect the stereotype of the adulterer as the arch-enemy, and likewise the arch-enemy of the moment as at least a potential adulterer.

One question remains to be answered. Was Epalanga a particularly rebellious, squabbling, divided, village, because of the presence of an unusual number of aggressive individuals? It is not possible to estimate the number of disputes per village, and the disputes which have been described were the most important of which I had personal knowledge. They were touched off by personal antagonisms rather than by structural contradictions. Yet they tie in with what has been said of the Umbundu social structure in earlier chapters to such a degree that they seem to reflect the lines along which any case of the sort would proceed. The weakness of the chiefs, stripped of traditional sanctions and lacking official confidences, the power-less prestige of the traditional headman, the lack of defined village unity, the role of the catechetical school and its officials, who have come to represent the village as a whole, the loosely structured yet stabilizing kinship system, all described in earlier chapters, have re-emerged as parts of a reasonably effective system of social control within which people quarrel and by which their quarrels are settled. It is possible for the villagers by appealing to patrons to check tyrannical behaviour on the part of chief and headmen and to get a fair hearing at the post. Within the local community disputants, once their anger has blown over, may be reunited by the ties of kinship and affinity.

CONCLUSIONS

The phrase 'A Study of Social Control and Social Change among the Ovimbundu' implies an analysis of the working of the social maintenance mechanism in a period of social change. The concept appears almost paradoxical since it seems that effective maintenance machinery[1] would prevent social change, and rapid social change is often associated by anthropologists with a situation of individual and social demoralization and disintegration.[2] At the present time the Ovimbundu of the area where fieldwork was done have undergone very rapid social change and have a reasonably effective system of social control, which, however, differs considerably from the traditional system. To confirm these statements, I briefly summarize the material provided in previous chapters.

In the time of the rubber trade (1874–1911) there existed a number of Umbundu kingdoms. The king, assisted and checked, as elsewhere in Africa by titled ministers, was responsible for external relations, undertook certain rituals, and provided a supreme court of appeal where trials were conducted by set rules of procedure. The real unit of law, as regards Gumba at least, seems to have been the sub-chiefdom, with its few thousand inhabitants, governed by a chief who like the king had to administer justice together with his councillors.

This body of councillors included the village headmen who were the heads of bodies of agnatic kin. They had general legal and political responsibility for the village. While the disputes arising in village relations were kept within the patrilineal kin group, the problems arising from the inheritance of movable goods and particularly from the highly important caravan trade were dealt with in the matrilineal group. Owing to the dispersed nature of this group and to its commercial preoccupations the sanctions operating within it must have differed somewhat from those found at the chief's court or village men's

---

[1] For this term see S. F. Nadel, *Theory of Social Structure*, London, 1957, p. 55.
[2] e.g. G. and M. Wilson, *Analysis of Social Change*, Cambridge, 1945.

house. Wealthy members who did not assist their kin were liable to be accused of sorcery. A mother's brother had the right to sell his sister's son as punishment for the latter's misconduct or to pay his own debts, a sanction counterbalancing the rights of the poorer matrilineal kin to receive loans without the obligation of repayment. As the matrilineal groups existed apparently across sub-chiefdom boundaries they formed a means of social control in those trading activities which provided the major focus of Umbundu interests and which flowed over the boundaries of the political groupings whose smallest unit was the patrilineally based village.

The disappearance of the matrilineal kin groups must be associated with the collapse of the old economy, and to judge from my difficulty in getting information about them their disintegration must have come about fairly rapidly after the end of the trade. Authority within the sub-chiefdom and village remained at a level fairly near the traditional norm till about 1935. After that social change has rapidly dissolved most of the traditional institutions.

The existing system of social control depends on political, local, and kinship systems very different from those previously operative. Cases are very often taken to the post without being previously taken to the chief. The latter's position is a combination of executive of the orders of the post (a role he shares with the government headman) with the surviving prestige represented by the skulls of his predecessors and the ministerial titles allocated to his kinsmen and associates. While the chief and government headmen may settle minor cases, they do not operate any system of courts by which disputes can be regularly and satisfactorily settled.

Judicial power has been effectively transferred from the indigenous society to the 'civilized' community and for a dispute to be brought to a settlement a decision must be obtained from some 'civilized' person or a negotiated arrangement may be made under threat of referring the matter to the post. Considerable importance therefore attaches to the mobilization of ties with some 'civilized' person who may be an employer but is most frequently the mission, which to some degree acts as a patron for all natives. Hence the local representatives of the mission, the catechist and elder of the school, tend to become the guardians of the public interest against arrogance on the part of the chief and government headmen.

In the conflict between the local representatives of the post and of the mission the latter are likely, if they have a good case, to win since they have a closer link with the mission than the chief and government headmen have with the post. While the policy of the administration of dissolving the indigenous political system has been highly successful it has not created new bureaucratic institutions at the local level, and the chief and government headmen have just sufficient power to do what the post tells them to do. The traditional headmen, while they still act as focuses of kin ties in a village have prestige rather than power; a prestige, however, sufficient to rally considerable support for them in a dispute. The catechetical school and its officials, represent the village to the outside world and provide what is nowadays the only institutional grouping on a village basis.

The role of the missions in social control is threefold; the establishment of new social groupings and forms of leadership at village level, the decision of disputes and the influencing of the *chefe's* decisions, and the giving of a feeling of approximation to the 'civilized' population. It is the missions rather than the chiefs and headmen who provide the main social bridges between the 'civilized' and native populations, since both groups participate in their institutions and values.[3]

The kinship system, whose operation must form an important part of any system of social control, has also undergone very great changes. The old kinship groups have disappeared, and the system is now cognatic, with little distinction between patrilateral and matrilateral kin although there is a certain matrilineal pull in choice of residence. Kinship norms have

[3] This does not deny the importance of the administration and the economy in linking the 'civilized' and natives together; yet this administrative and economic integration does not provide the sense of community which to a limited degree is given through the missions, which also provide the only opportunity for individual natives to have influence in a social sphere beyond the range of kin and neighbours; in the Catholic missions by the provision of an influential patron, in the Protestant Native Church by participation in Church councils and courts.

become confused and vague; the existence of a kinship tie provides an opportunity to build a social relation rather than a jural obligation to fulfil certain duties. With the disappearance of the commensality which marked the patrilineal kin, and the economic co-operation characteristic of the matrilineal groups, the elementary family has emerged as the primary domestic and economic grouping.

In this rather amorphous system, coherence is given by the marriage tie. The very high rate of preferential marriages creates a great number of affinal (and subsequently kinship) ties within a limited area, and it seems to be from this that the neighbourhood community derives its cohesion. At the level of the individual marriage (as opposed to that of the total structure) the relation between husband and wife is a very close one, with, conversely, the relation between a man and his wife's lover being the archetype of hostility.

It is now necessary to see how the description of the two systems of social control relate to the problems of the social changes which have intervened to turn into the other. Obviously social change has been very great. It is not perhaps possible to point to any one factor responsible for the speed of the process. The old political system would not have disintegrated if the administration had used it as the intermediary between it and the natives. However, the hostility of the administration to the chiefs has not succeeded in all parts of Angola in breaking down traditional authority.[4]

Economic change has certainly affected very considerably the social structure. In other parts of Africa a cash economy gained by selling crops and working for wages has replaced a subsistence economy where exchanges were made by barter and gift exchanges. The Ovimbundu were experienced traders used to a currency and with a business-like, rather grasping outlook.[5] Through the matrilineal groups this commercial activity was fitted into the kinship system. The disappearance of the trade brought a sharp fall in the Umbundu standard of living and destroyed the need for developed credit facilities. Instead of the

---

[4] Among the Ngangela of the area round Vila Artur de Paiva the chiefs retain their authority.

[5] See Serpa Pinto, pp. 169–71 and F. S. Arnot, *Garenganze*, London, 1889, p. 116.

gaining of wealth by means involving extensive economic co-operation among the Ovimbundu themselves, money was earned in an individual relation to a particular European whether planter or trader.

It must be recognized that the relation between economic change and the continuation or disintegration of kinship groups is a yet unsolved problem of anthropology,[6] particularly as it is seldom possible to isolate the economic pressure. I emphasize the readiness of the Ovimbundu for change, their willing acceptance of the role of clients to the whites.[7] It may be suggested that this attitude was established in the period of the trade when the Ovimbundu were ultimately dependent on the whites for trade goods and that this attitude of imitation and receptivity lies behind the disappearance of so much of the old social structure and the lack of any myth of, or even interest in, the past.[8]

I have claimed that the present system of social control is effective.[9] This may be granted empirically for the reasons already given, the absence of serious crime or prolonged conflict involving the whole community, the effective checks on the functionaries of the post, and the failure of squabbles to tear the network of kin and affinal ties. If a working social system is a proof of an integrated society, then contemporary Umbundu society qualifies for this description. This is not the only possible way of looking at it. It may be claimed that under present circumstances the Ovimbundu are no longer integrated by their tribal system but are held together by the Angolan

[6] For various comments on this problem see A. I. Richards, in *African Systems of Kinship and Marriage*, p. 251, M. Fortes, 'Structure of Unilineal Descent Groups', in *American Anthropologist*, Feb. 1953, M. Douglas (review of Mitchell's *The Yao Village*) in *Africa*, July 1957.

[7] Cf. the Ngangela name for the Ovimbundu, the Ovimbali, a term traditionally applied to Africans living in close contact with the whites. The Ovimbundu accept this stereotype.

[8] 'A lack of history is correlated with the amorphous character of the society.' E. Colson in Colson and Gluckman (ed.) *Seven Tribes of British Central Africa*, Oxford, 1951, p. 100.

[9] Other quarrels of which I heard while in Epalanga: a messenger from the mission sent to intervene in a marriage dispute was attacked; the chief of Chicunda summoned to the mission for a telling-off after beating up one of his people; a man from Gumba refusing to go to a funeral in Cassongue of a man whose death he was thought to have caused by sorcery.

Government,[10] which has deprived them of all legal and political autonomy. The present Umbundu social system deprived of any form of public life ticks over, as a man who has been paralysed may continue to live. The cultural barriers and structural gulf between the post, the basic unit of the administration, and the people, are to a certain extent bridged by the mission. This task throws a considerable strain on the organizations set up by the missions, to which they are far from equal.[11] The common values shared by 'civilized' and native, whose introduction was ascribed to the missions, give the Ovimbundu psychological compensation rather than a genuine participation in the culture of the ruling group. The stability which marks social relations in the area is passivity rather than integration.

The most truthful approach would seem to be a synthesis of the two arguments. The disintegration of the old legal and political institutions and the attitude of dependence and passivity towards Europeans cohere with a stability provided by the pattern of kin and affinal ties and the continuity of local relations. It has been argued that the range of marriages (and hence the range of kinship ties) has not noticeably expanded in recent years, and that the links which orient Gumba to the north and west rather than to the south and east date back to the nineteenth century. Such other factors as the poor local communications, the limited economic development of the area, and the absence of resident whites in Gumba may also have helped to preserve the continuity and security of the 'private' life of individuals.[12] In other areas of Umbundu country, especially near the railway line, where communications are easy, Europeans and *assimilados* are numerous, and there are more marked differences of wealth, this 'coherence' of change and continuity may have very much less empirical efficiency.

In one part of Umbundu country in 1955, a contra-accultura-

[10] Putting it another way; there is no Umbundu political system, and hence the nearest approach to Umbundu politics are the squabbles of Chapter IX.

[11] The missionaries complain of the poor calibre of many catechists, and the catechists complain of the lack of obedience of their people.

[12] The relations between two individuals may remain friendly, even though the form of their relations changes.

tive movement arose which combined features found in cargo-cults and anti-witchcraft campaigns,[13] social activities usually regarded as products of a malaise in the relations between Europeans and an indigenous society.[14] The Ovimbundu whom I knew were not ready to take the initiative in their dealings with the 'civilized' population; but it would be wrong to regard the system of social control that I have tried to describe as being true for much more than a very small area of Umbundu country and a very limited extent of time.

[13] The movement began at Bela Vista on the railway line and spread over south-eastern Umbundu country into the Ngangela area. Its leaders were men and women who called themselves saints and claimed to have died and come to life again. They announced that all sorcery would cease, and those who continued it would die in an unusual way. They forbade the wearing of black clothes and ordered the killing of black livestock (fowls and pigs). They also forbade the growing of maize for sale. It was stated that rain would come from heaven to kill the whites (according to some accounts only the bad whites) and the blacks would then have their goods. This movement was spread through the catechetical schools. It was eventually repressed by administrative action. Private information. Also article in *O Apostolado*, Luanda, Oct. 27, 1956.

[14] See A. I. Richards, 'A Modern Movement of Witchfinders', *Africa*, Oct. 1935.

BIBLIOGRAPHY OF THE
OVIMBUNDU SINCE 1900

ALVES, ALBINO. *Dicionário Etimológico Bundo-Portugués*, Lisbon, 1951. 'Parabola Bunda do Mes de Outubro' in *Portugal em Africa* (Lisbon), May–June 1952, pp. 193–196; September–October 1952, pp. 500–505.

BASTOS, AUGUSTO. 'Traços Geraes sobre a Etnografia do Districto de Benguella'. Series of Articles in *Boletim de Sociedade de Geografia de Lisboa*, 1908.
'Monografia de Catumbella'. Series of Articles in *Boletim de Sociedade de Geografia de Lisboa*, 1910. Both these studies have been published in book form but are not easily accessible.

BAUMANN, H. 'Die Frage der Steinbauten und Steingraber in Angola', *Paideuma*. April 1956, pp. 118–51.

BELL, W. C. Umbundu Tales, *Journal of American Folklore*, 1922.

CASTRO JUNIOR, AUGUSTO. 'Indigenas do Bie' *Mensário Administrativo* (Luanda), September–October, 1950.

CASTRO JUNIOR, AUGUSTO CONTOS, 'Lendas e Proverbios "Umbundo" Concelho do Bie', *Mensário Administrativo* 13: September 1948.

CHATELAIN, A. *Heli Chatelain, l'Ami de l'Angola* (Lausanne, 1918).

CHILDS, G. M. *Umbundu Kinship and Character*, Oxford, 1949.
'The Church in Angola: a few impressions'. *International Review of Missions*, April 1958.
'The Peoples of Angola in the Seventeenth Century according to Cadornega'. *Journal of African History*, Vol. I, No. 2, 1960, pp. 271–9.

CUSHMAN, M. F. *Missionary Doctor in Africa*, New York, 1944.

ENNIS, ELIZABETH. 'Women's Names among the Ovimbundu of Angola', *African Studies* (Johannesburg), March 1945.

ESTERMANN, C. 'Clans et Alliances entre Clans dans le Sud-Ouest de l'Angola', *Anthropos*, May–August 1952.

EVAMBI, R. K., translated by Ennis, M. W. 'The Marriage Customs of the Ovimbundu', *Africa*, July 1938.

FERNANDES, MARIO, 'Concelho de Huambo, Esquema de Historia de Sambo'. *Mensário Administrativo*, March–April 1952.

HAMBLY, W. D. *The Ovimbundu of Angola*, Chicago, 1934.

HASTINGS, D. A. *Ovimbundu Beliefs and Practices*, 1933 (Ph.D. thesis Typescript).

KEILING, LUIZ. *Quarenta Anos de Africa*, Braga, 1934.

McCULLOCH, MERRAN. *The Ovimbundu of Angola* (Ethnographic Survey of Africa), London 1952.

NEVINSON, H. W. *A Modern Slavery*, New York, 1906.

SANTOS BRANDAO, ANIBAL DOS. Articles in *Mensário Administrativo*, March–April, July–August 1950, and September–October, November–December 1952.

SARMENTO, ALEXANDRO. Contribuição para o Estudo das Mutilaçoes Etnicas dos Indigenas de Angola (Huambo and Sambo) *Trabalhos de Anthropologia e Ethnologia*, 1951.

STRANGEWAYS, ALICE K. 'The advance of African women in Angola', in *African Women*, July 1956.

TUCKER, J. T. *Drums in the Darkness*, Toronto and New York, 1927.
Angola, Land of the Blacksmith Prince, London, 1933.
Currie of Chissamba, Toronto, 1945.
A short article in Notes and News in *Africa*, April 1956.

TUCKER, L. S. 'The Divining Basket of the Ovimbundu', *Journal of the Royal Anthropological Institute*, 1940.

VALENTE, JOAQUIM. 'Conceito de Doença e Cura em Caconda e Bailundo', in *Portugal em Africa*, November–December 1948.

VALENTE, JOSE, F. 'A Familia Indigena do Planalto de Benguela, *Portugal em Africa*, November–December 1949.

VERLY, R. 'Le "Roi Divin" chez les Ovimbundu et Kimbundu de l'Angola', *Zaïre*, June 1956.

BIBLIOGRAPHY OF THE OVIMBUNDU BEFORE 1900

Annaes do Conselho Ultramarino, Lisbon, 1854–61, 1st Volume. Descripção de Viagem Feita de Loanda em 1845 by J. R. Graca. Uma Viagem de Angola em Direcção a Contra Costa by Silva Porto.

Angola; Viagem Feita a Caconda by J. J. Liborio.
Noticia do Sertão do Balundo by C. de A. Sandoval.

Annaes Maritimos Coloniaes, Lisbon 1844–1846. 4th Volume Descripção da Capitania de Benguella (1799), 5th Volume Noticia da Cidade de Benguella e dos costumes dos Gentios Habitantes daquelle Sertão by Pinheiro de Lacerda.

ARNOT, F. S. *Garenganze*, London, 1889.
  Bihe and Garenganze, London, 1893.
Benguella, Relatorios do Districto de. For 1887 and 1891, Lisbon.

CAPELLO, H. and IVENS, R. *From Benguella to the Territory of Yacca*, London, 1882.

CAMERON, V. L. *Across Africa*, London, 1877.

DELGADO, RALPH, *Ao Sul de Cuanza*, Lisbon, 1944.

DIAS DE CARVALHO, H. *Etnografia e Historia Tradicional dos Povos de Lunda*, Lisbon, 1890.

JOHNSON, J. *Reality versus Romance in South Central Africa*, New York, 1893.

LABAT, J. B. *Relation Historique de l'Etiopie Occidentale*, Paris, 1732. (A translation of Cavazzi.)

MAGYAR, L. *Reisen in Sud-Afrika*, Leipzig and Pest, 1859.

Missionary Herald, 1880–1900 (Boston U.S.A.).

MONTEIRO, J. J. *Angola and the River Congo*, London, 1875.

PAIVA, ARTUR DE. *Excerptos dos Seus Jornais*, Lisbon, 1940.

PAIVA COUCEIRO, HENRIQUE DE. *Relatorio de Viagem entre Bailundo e as Terras de Mucusso*, Lisbon, 1892.

RAVENSTEIN (Ed.). *The Strange Adventures of Andrew Battell*, London, 1901.

SERPA PINTO, A. *How I Crossed Africa*, London, 1881.

SILVA PORTO, A. F. F. A series of articles in the *Boletim de Sociedade de Geografia de Lisboa*, 1885–6.

VALDEZ, F. TRAVASSOS. *Six Years of a Traveller's Life in Western Africa*, London, 1864.

BIBLIOGRAPHY OF OTHER
WORKS OF SIGNIFICANCE

CERQUEIRA, IVO DE. *Vida Social Indigena na Colonia de Angola*, Lisbon, 1947.

DUFFY, JAMES. *Portuguese Africa*, Harvard, 1959.

EGERTON, F. CLEMENT C. *Angola in Perspective*, London, 1957.

ESTERMANN, C. *Etnografia do Sudoeste de Angola*
  Vol. I, Lisbon, 1956.

  Vol. II, Lisbon, 1957.
  Vol. III (forthcoming).
  (See reviews in *Africa,* July 1958 and April 1959.)

FREYRE, GILBERTO. *Aventura e Rotina*, Lisbon, 1953.

GALVAO, H. and SELVAGEM, C. *Imperio Ultramarino Portugués*, Vol. III, Angola, Lisbon, 1952.

HAILEY, LORD. *An African Survey Revised*, 1956, Oxford, 1956.

LANG, A., and TASTEVIN, C. *La Tribu des Va-Nyaneka*, Corbeil, 1937.

McCULLOCH. *The Southern Lunda and Related Peoples.* (Ethnographic Survey of Africa), London, 1951.

MARQUARDSEN, H. and STAHL, A. *Angola*, Berlin, 1928.

INDEX

INDEX

Fines, xvi, 14, 17, 31, 111–12, 115, 141–2, 147
Fishing, 48, 66–7
Funerals, 13–14, 38, 51, 60, 62, 71, 82, 86, 106, 121–2, 159

Genealogies, 51–2, 105, 107–8, 111
Gumba, geography of, xvii, 29, 89, 113, 160; — history of, 13 35–8, 160; — reputation of, xvii, 72, 77

Hambly, W. D., xv, 16, 90, 92
Hamlets, 22, 48, 77, 84
Hanya, 6, 7
Hastings, D. A., xv, xvii, 11, 13–14, 16–17, 92–3, 100, 164
Headmen, government, 39, 43–5, 72, 82, 87, 89, 128, 133–6, 150–2, 154; — traditional, 39, 43, 45–7, 49, 58–61, 63, 64, 67, 128, 149–50
History, African ideas of, xvi, 4, 159
Huambo, kingdom of, 12
Hunters, 107, 121
Hunts, 44, 47, 48, 50

Inheritance, 99, 106–7, 155

Jagas, 1, 2, 4, 7, 13
Johannesburg, 30

Kamundongo, xv
Kimbundu, xv, 4, 82, 88, 113
Kingdoms, 3–5, 7–8, 11, 14, 18–19, 100, 155
Kings, 4–5, 7, 11, 13–14, 37, 68, 100, 155
Kinship system, modern, 61–4, 100–111, 126, 153–4, 157–9;—traditional, xvii, 14–17, 92–100, 108–110, 111–15, 155–6
Kinship terms, 84, 93–6
Kwanyama, 30, 67–8, 72

Labour, contract, 23, 37, 59, 71–2, 77–8, 101, 115, 120, 129, 147–8; — voluntary, 23, 72, 101, 109
Liga Nacional Africana, 26
Livestock, 14, 67, 70, 73, 104, 121, 161
Lobito, 21, 25
Luanda, 25, 26, 30

Luba, 10
Lunda, Northern, 2, 10;—Southern, see Ndembu

Marriage, 17, 48, 50–2, 56–8, 66, 87, 101, 111–27, 129–30, 153, 160
Matrikin, 15, 16, 18, 51, 62, 74, 92–3, 99, 103, 105–8, 112, 114, 155–9
Meals, 15, 56, 99, 115, 120–3, 143
Ministers, of king, 2, 8, 12–13, 41–2, 59, 147, 149–50, 155–6
Missions, Catholic, 5, 6, 23, 27–8, 76, 83, 87, 156
Mother–child tie, 98, 100, 124–5
Mother's brother–sister's son tie, 17–18, 61–2, 103, 110, 124, 156
Mutual aid, 16, 73–4, 100, 108–9
Mwekalia, 2, 12–13, 37, 87, 140, 148
Mystical sanctions, 115, 121–2, 143

Natal, 30
Ndembu, 4, 74
Ndjandju, 13, 82, 104
Nganda, 6, 7
Nova Lisboa, xv, 21, 129; — Bishop of, 87–8
Nyaneka-Humbi, 2, 6

Olongoya, 7, 29, 112
ondjango, 15, 64, 99, 119
Ovimbali, xv, 7, 159
Ovimbundu, xi, xv, 2–3, 5, 7, 10–11, 19, 21, 24, 32, 85, 88–9, 112, 118, 155, 159–60

Pagans, 42, 77–8, 85–6, 88–9, 118, 121, 143
Patrikin, 15–16, 51, 92–102, 105, 108–9, 112, 114–15
Plantations, 10, 22–3, 30, 72, 78, 101
Ploughs, 74
Police, 35, 39–40, 81, 101, 129
Portugal, 21, 23, 31
Portuguese customs, 7, 9, 84, 120
posto, chefes de, 24, 31, 38–40, 84, 87, 130, 146–8, 150–2, 157
Posts, administrative, 23, 35, 72, 80–1, 120, 129, 134–6, 152–4, 159
Protestants, Protestantism, 24–5, 27–8, 31, 73, 82, 88, 124

168